A Rainbow Book

John D. MacArthur

A View From The Bar

(A Memoir)

Bob Sanford

With warmest Regards!
Bob Sanford

Library of Congress Cataloging-in-Publication Data

Sanford, Bob, 1940-
    John D. MacArthur, a view from the bar : a memoir / Bob Sanford.
       p.   cm.
    Includes bibliographical references (p.).
    ISBN 1-56825-036-3 (alk. paper)
    1. MacArthur, John D., 1897-1978. 2. Capitalists and financiers-
-United States--Biography. I. Title.
HG172.M28S26   1996
647.759'32--dc20
[B]   96-18335
                                          CIP

John D. MacArthur: A View From the Bar (A Memoir)
Copyright 1996 © Bob Sanford

Published by Rainbow Books, Inc.
P. O. Box 430
Highland City, FL 33846-0430
Editorial Offices Telephone (941) 648-4420
Orders: Telephone (800) 356-9315, Fax (800) 242-0036

Cover and interior design by Betsy A. Lampé.
Cover portrait by Burton Silverman © Burton Silverman.
Back cover photo by Marc J. Hagemeir. Used with permission.

Manufactured in the United States of America

DEDICATION

To the Master of the Game and all the Players among us.

Contents

Acknowledgments

My special thanks to these people who took their time to help with this book:

Molly Campany, Palm Beach Shores, FL; Arthur Lee Cooper, West Palm Beach, FL; Peter Swanberg, The Tux Shop, Palm Beach Gardens, FL; Bob Ratcliffe, Sr., Palm Beach Shores, FL; Thomas C. Chilcote, Mayor of Palm Beach Shores, FL; J. D. Davy, North Palm Beach, FL; Carolyn Gray, West Palm Beach, FL; Jane Brown, Juno Beach, FL; Lonnie Cargill, Lake Park, FL; Ray Boyer, John D. and Catherine T. MacArthur Foundation, Chicago, IL; Patricia Smith, Palm Beach Gardens, FL, Mary Dymon, North Palm Beach, FL; Paula Lucas, Jupiter, FL, Joe Lemay, Palm Beach Gardens, FL, and Ted Prior, John D. and Catherine T. MacArthur Foundation, Palm Beach Gardens, FL.

My special thanks also go to the following for the use of photos and illustrations and sculpture:

Molly Campany, Palm Beach Shores, FL; Bob Ratcliffe, Sr., Palm Beach Shores, FL; Mayor Thomas C. Chilcote, Mayor of Palm Beach Shores, FL; Dennis and Frank De Cesare,

North Palm Beach, FL; Sara Mugavero, 60-Minutes Photo, North Palm Beach, FL; Ray Boyer, John D. and Catherine T. MacArthur Foundation, Chicago, IL; Susan Benson, Benson Signs, Riviera Beach, FL; Margo McMahon, Chicago, IL; Bill Wood, West Palm Beach, FL; Bobbie Lemay, Palm Beach Gardens, FL; Felipe A. Catasus, Lake Park, FL; and Burton Silverman, New York, NY.

Chapter 1

Inside John D. MacArthur

Just recently, I went to Florida's North Palm Beach Library to hear Patrick Smith, a well-known author, speak about his writing. After his talk he held an open forum, wherein he asked for questions and comments about writing experiences. I raised my hand and was acknowledged. Suddenly I found myself on my feet, saying, "I've just written my first book."

Mr. Smith said, "Well, what did you choose to write about, young man?"

Such flattery — I'm no longer *that* young — evidently got to me, since I responded, "I chose to write about a man who I admired more than any individual I've met. I chose to write about a man who — back in the 1920s had empty pockets and by the mid-1970s was the second richest man in these United States of America. I chose to write about a man who lived with his wife in an apartment atop a hotel — not far from where we all sit this afternoon — that's since been torn down over on Palm Beach Shores. The name of that hotel was the Colonnades Beach Hotel, and that man's name was John Donald MacArthur."

Sighs rippled around the room, bringing a smile to my face. For in spite of those who might simply refer to John D.

MacArthur as an S.O.B., there are many others who saw a great deal more in my profile of a multi-billionaire. It is my opinion that John D. MacArthur proved to all mankind that in the land of opportunity, if a person is willing to work long and hard to achieve a chosen goal, putting aside sharkskin suits and shiny new cars, the overall rewards are limitless . . . This is that story, as I know it, much of it on a personal level as an employee of John D. MacArthur.

When John D. MacArthur came on the Florida scene in the late 1950s — already a rich man — it was pretty much virgin territory. John and his wife Catherine lived in Lake Park, just north of West Palm Beach on Evergreen Drive. Confident his insurance empire was doing well, MacArthur now turned his attention to real estate. Over the years he spent much of his time purchasing property all over Florida. At one point, he owned 100,000 acres of land in Florida and was the state's largest land owner.

In 1963, when MacArthur purchased the Colonnades Beach Hotel in Palm Beach Shores on Singer Island, the MacArthurs moved into the apartments they had built on top of the Paradise Building there. MacArthur later told me that when he came to Palm Beach Shores, he saw a tiny, sleepy, uneventful town. He figured he might just raise a little hell and give these people something to talk about.

MacArthur had no regard for building permits, blueprints and things of that nature. Therefore, these apartments were built from rough drafts, and he hired the cheapest labor he could find to complete the task. The overall construction was shoddy at best.

As for the Colonnades Beach Hotel, it was a sight to behold. A maze of buildings connected by countless arched breezeways gave the hotel its name. Built in 1949 by architect A. O. Edwards, who designed Palm Beach Shores, it

John D. MacArthur

Permission: Ray Boyer, John D. and Catherine T.
MacArthur Foundation, Chicago, Illinois (1976).

**Front view of main building
of the Colonnades Beach Hotel.**

Property of Bob Sanford (1978).

**Rear view of main building of the Colonnades Beach Hotel.
The Bob Hope Suite is at the very top.**

Property of Bob Sanford (1978).

started as a much smaller hotel, known as Inlet Court. When MacArthur purchased it for $750,000, he promoted it to attract international tours. In its heyday in the 1960s and 1970s, it had more than 400 rooms, and the Colonnades was the place to be seen — such celebrities as Bob Hope, Jackie Gleason, Jack Nicklaus, Paul Harvey, Lee Trevino, and more, all frequenting the premises.

Meanwhile, long lines of people from all over the world — entrepreneurs, real estate tycoons, bankers, brokers —

would form a line in the lobby of the Colonnades just for a chance to talk with John D. MacArthur in his "office", which was, in reality, a small table in the hotel coffee shop. With any kind of luck, these folks might even see MacArthur go out and feed his beloved ducks.

Since MacArthur was something of a pack rat, his hotel was full of collectibles — china, huge crystal chandeliers, and a life-sized hand-carved sleigh from Imperial Poland with a horse in flight that sat in the lobby. The hotel also featured a carousel bar which rotated once an hour, a championship swimming pool, and a three-tiered dining room laid out around a large saltwater fish tank. On the back lawn were beautiful waterfalls with colored lights shining on them.

Probably the best remembered part of the hotel is the penthouse MacArthur built on top of the sixth floor of the main building. He named it The Bob Hope Suite, and used it to lure Hope away from Palm Beach. The Colonnades didn't have a Palm Beach address, but it had ambiance, character and charm.

Throughout all of this, the town politicians fought MacArthur with a vengeance but to no avail. As if this wasn't enough, in the years 1967-1968, his outdoor game show, Treasure Island, produced by MacArthur Productions, infuriated everyone. The small quiet hamlet was now bustling with buses and cars, people eager to be part of this extravaganza. The half-hour show aired on ABC-TV and was hosted by John Bartholomew Tucker. MacArthur had special lagoons built for the show behind the Paradise Building. The hubbub was almost too much for the people of Palm Beach Shores. They hated this interruption in their sedate existence. Fortunately, for them, the show only lasted one year.

MacArthur meant no harm by it all. He saw possibilities, while the town didn't want to change. But MacArthur got a real kick out of stirring the boiling kettle.

Thus, Florida became MacArthur's cup of tea. And nothing and no one could stand in his way. He was determined, as determined a man as I have ever met. Of course, I did not meet MacArthur until he was 77 years old. But it was all there, that determination, perhaps from the day he was born.

It is difficult for anyone to figure out the inner workings of another person. So, for me to try and figure out a man as complex as John D. MacArthur is a waste. But having spent much time observing Mr. MacArthur in a working relationship, I have formed some basic conclusions about him.

MacArthur was undoubtedly tight-fisted, so tight-fisted that he'd return a cola bottle for its deposit himself. But he was a world-class businessman; and that is not just my opinion. It has been reported that Howard Hughes considered MacArthur the hardest of men to beat in a business deal. Coming from Hughes, this was a great compliment indeed.

One incident that occurred between these two high-powered business adversaries is particularly enlightening . . .

MacArthur was staying in one of the hotels he owned in Chicago. Directly across the street was a hotel owned by Howard Hughes and atop that hotel was a flashing neon light that disturbed the sleep of MacArthur in his room. Quick tempered, MacArthur picked up the phone by his bed, called Hughes' hotel and demanded to speak with Hughes.

When Howard Hughes finally came on the line, John proceeded to tell Howard of his complaint in no uncertain terms.

Hughes loved this; he was annoying a fierce competitor. "There's nothing I can do about it," he responded smoothly. "That's my sign. It's there. And it's going to stay there. And it's going to flash. That's my way of advertising."

"Well," said MacArthur, "that's just fine with me. When

I get back to Florida, I'll draw up papers and buy the hotel!"
And that's exactly what he did.

Certainly MacArthur didn't need another hotel. He just
wanted to show Hughes who was boss.

However, one imagines that MacArthur didn't short-
change Hughes. MacArthur once said, "A good deal to be a
good deal has to be a good deal for both sides."

Unlike Howard Hughes or even John Paul Getty,
MacArthur was never remote or reclusive. He was a very
public man, always there at his table, almost always accessible.

For instance, if you were fortunate enough to have the
opportunity of sitting at his table in the little coffee shop at
the Colonnades Beach Hotel to discuss whatever deal you had
in mind, chances are you'd already been to Florida banks
throughout the area and failed to acquire the kind of money
you needed. Therefore, having heard of this multi-billionaire
on Singer Island, you figured you might as well give him a
shot at loaning you money.

So far as MacArthur was concerned, he didn't care if your
proposition involved a new product you'd just invented, a real
estate deal, whatever. He listened, and if you knew what you
were talking about, and if it was a good deal for all involved,
then you walked out of the Colonnades with the money to
accomplish what you'd set out to do.

Of course, such ventures never went without advice and
the stiff terms on which the loan was being made. In fact, it
was imperative that one listen, since final decisions were
evidently based on your ability, not only to speak clearly and
plainly about your needs and why they were important, but
also to learn at the master's knee.

That done, it was really a simple matter. A handshake,
and within the next 24 hours, MacArthur's attorneys would
make sure you had the money.

Of course, that didn't mean the money was handed over without restraints. When a due date came around for MacArthur to get paid, if you didn't pay up, you found you owed him, not only what was due, but an added 20 percent. And if that didn't work, MacArthur's lawyers were on your doorstep the next day to foreclose.

Many people, imagining a man like MacArthur with his vast wealth wouldn't be so harsh — though they had been told in advance and in no uncertain terms about their responsibilities and the penalties involved — were surprised by his actions, and personal grudges and complaints to MacArthur were not all that unusual. But MacArthur retorted by saying, "What do you think a bank would have done under the same circumstances? Don't you think they would have foreclosed on you? You're damn right they would have. What kind of a business man would I be, if I didn't look out for my interests? Not a good businessman at all."

As the beverage manager at the Colonnades Beach Hotel, I watched in awe as employees vied for time off. For instance, if you went to MacArthur and explained that you needed some time off to make some money in some type of deal you were working on, he'd grant you time off. But if you went to him and said, "Gee, Mr. MacArthur, I haven't had any time off in my life, and my whole family is after me to spend some time with them on a little trip for a couple of days," MacArthur would cock his head in disbelief.

Typical of this kind of situation happened around eight o'clock one morning, just after I'd come into the hotel. MacArthur was running around in a frenzy, trying to find the head chef. He accosted me and demanded to know where he was.

"I don't know, sir. I just got in, and I haven't been into the kitchen yet."

MacArthur went off muttering under his breath.

The next time MacArthur came my way that morning, he was talking to Ron Kairalla, who I always called Mr. K. Mr. K had just arrived on the job, and MacArthur was yelling at him, "Where's the head chef?"

"Don't worry," said Mr. K. "I'll find him."

About fifteen minutes later I walked by MacArthur's table in the coffee shop. Mr. K was telling MacArthur, "I called the chef at his home. He told me he won't be coming in today. He was going to call in a couple of minutes. His wife is having a baby today."

"Bullshit," snapped MacArthur. "You get his ass in here right now. His wife is having the baby — not him."

Which brings up another point about MacArthur — loyalty. I sometimes think the man honored loyalty over most other virtues. He expected unvarnished loyalty from his employees at the Colonnades Beach Hotel. Later, when I spoke with those who worked for his Bankers Life and Casualty in Chicago, I discovered the same was true there. Yes, loyalty was a virtue. In fact, in my many interviews for this book, I discovered most people who knew MacArthur well spoke of him as if he might be larger than life itself, as if they had always looked up to the man. In other words, he commanded respect, not just because he had vast riches and power, but because he was a man of his word and loyalty ran two ways.

Yes, John D. MacArthur was a complex man. But despite his penchant for loyalty and his reputation for being tough as nails in a business deal, he could be warm and understanding. I suspect he was often misread by those who failed to take him seriously or those who tried to engineer a deal with him.

On October 28, 1957, *The Chicago American,* ran an article saying, "Unlike 54 of the 76 richest Americans who either inherited their money or made it in oil where taxes give investors a break, MacArthur was born poor and was flat broke 20 years ago."

Informed that he was one of 22 self-made "non-oil multimillionaires", MacArthur quipped, "That's nice. At least it sets me aside from the guys whose Poppas gave it to them. My old man was poor."

According to sources very close to me, in 1976, MacArthur said, "The story about me should not be written while I am alive. I am a very busy man, and I have many good things to do. If the story is written about me, it should be long after I'm gone, and the author should talk about the good things I have done in my life."

And what good had he done with his life?

Not only did MacArthur provide opportunities for others while he lived, his wealth was left to posterity. He and his wife Catherine are perhaps the most unheralded philanthropists of our century.

The John D. and Catherine T. MacArthur Foundation, a reflection of the accumulation of vast wealth, is a private, independent, grant-making foundation dedicated to charity and public service. It has developed a limited number of programs in areas where it believes philanthropic effort can make an important contribution. Currently there are eight programs:

Community Initiatives Programs, which support cultural and community activities in Chicago, Illinois, and Palm Beach County, Florida;

Education Program for the development of literacy, numeracy, and critical and creative thinking skills;

General Program for special initiatives in media projects;

Health Program, devoted primarily to research on mental health and the biology of parasitic diseases;

MacArthur Fellows Program, which awards grants to exceptionally creative individuals in a wide range of endeavors;

Program on Peace and International Cooperation, which seeks to expand and strengthen the field of international security studies and to increase public understanding of complex security issues;

Population Program, focusing on women's reproductive health, and the relationship between population and the environment; and

World Environment and Resource Program, which supports conservation, public education and policy studies relating to key environment issues in the tropics.

To date, the foundation has given away approximately $800 million in grants. About $158 million has been devoted to the study of mental health, second only to the National Institute of Mental Health in Washington, DC. More than $92 million has been committed to studies of acid rain, preservation of rain forests, greenhouse warming . . . The MacArthur Fellows, which grants no-strings-attached funds to scientists, artists, writers, poets, musicians, you name it, to give these people the freedom they require to pursue excellence, awards large grants to such people every year. In fact, you can't listen to National Public Radio or watch television's Public Broadcasting System (PBS) without hearing or seeing the name of the foundation as a sponsor of many fine programs. And this is just to mention a few items with which you might identify. In truth, the foundation's assets are remarkable; recent figures show the value of the foundation at $3.2 billion.

What's most refreshing about the John D. and Catherine T. MacArthur Foundation is this: One need not apply; the foundation is not up for grabs. Each year a 12-member board quietly seeks out those areas and people that should be encouraged in providing the excellence required for a better world in which to live; then, the foundation announces who gets what.

John E. Corbally never knew MacArthur. But in his annual report on the foundation in 1988, as outgoing foundation president, perhaps he best understood MacArthur with these words:

"He found fun and excitement and satisfaction in making money, and he has provided us with the same kind of fun, excitement and satisfaction in permitting us to 'give it away'."

Praise for the man has ranged from "public spirited" (*Collier's* magazine) to MacArthur's soft spot for the handicapped and how many handicapped people he employed (*Look* magazine) to "refreshingly honest" (*Fortune* magazine).

John D. MacArthur and Bob Hope at the Colonnades Beach Hotel, Palm Beach Shores, Florida.

Permission: Bill Wood (early 1970s).

Chapter 2

An Overview of the MacArthur Family

Before I begin my memoir of days spent in the company of John D. MacArthur, it is well that you should know a bit about his background. Perhaps this will assist you in understanding him as we interact at the Colonnades Beach Hotel.

The original home of the MacArthurs was Scotland. The Clan MacArthur was an important branch of the Clan Campbell and was historically located in the region extending from Loch Awe to Lock Fyne in Argyllshire. A folk saying of the western highlands affirms the family's antiquity:

"There is nothing older unless the hills MacArthur and the devil."

William MacArthur was only 21-years-old in 1882 when he came to Manitoba, Canada, to serve as a lay preacher. William was a striking man with strong features, very black hair and a closely clipped black beard. Despite his poverty, he always maintained a dignified bearing and a proper appearance, while keeping his mind in equally good order. In fact, he worked to improve the scope and depth of his knowledge by reading religious literature and thus became acquainted with the newest translations of the Bible.

Once William joined the Christian Alliance, he never considered another path. His days of wandering from denomination to denomination were over. His life as a preacher, evangelist and Bible teacher were just beginning.

The Christian Alliance was largely a lay movement and its zealous men and women, along with a handful of clergy, spread far and wide. Soon William met a lovely woman and fell in love. Her name was Georgiana. She was the daughter of Alfred and Margaret Welstead. The Welsteads were part of a great 19th Century migration from the British Isles to Canada; and in 1893, Georgiana and William were married. After the vows, the couple departed for their new homestead in Saskatchewan, where William had filed for a land grant.

William had picked the perfect wife. Though gifted intellectually, Georgiana was kindhearted, fun-loving and cultured; and she looked forward to starting a home of her own on the frontier with her distinguished new husband. Resourceful, Georgiana adjusted readily to the harsh new land, and in due time she gave birth to seven children — Alfred, Margaret, Lawrence Telfer, Roderick, Helen, Charles and John.

Georgiana took everything in stride, never complaining. She had a true, on-going pioneer spirit, until she died of cancer on February 25, 1915.

As the years passed, William took his preaching everywhere. He was a popular speaker and Bible teacher known for his "hell, fire and brimstone" services, often preaching to audiences that reached 6,000 people. But in many places he found needs and no money to meet them. A storefront church required a building of its own; a church needed repairs; a congregation wanted a new wing on its church . . . But no obstacle was too large for William — not with a son like John. William explained that his son John was gloriously blessed in his business enterprises and would certainly want to give some of it back to the Lord. When William returned from these

**The William A. MacArthur family, circa 1901,
John D. MacArthur, center of front row.**

Permission: John D. and Catherine T. MacArthur Foundation

churches, he would explain to John the need and tell him of the promises he had made on John's behalf.

John was always quick to remind his father that he could not build a business by giving away huge sums of money. Whereupon William would shake his finger vigorously under his son's nose and say in a commanding voice, "I prayed that God would make you rich so you could help people, and now that he's done it, don't you forget it!"

John, always amused by his father's admonishment, would occasionally donate money to his father's causes. Still and all, he was no easy target, not even for his father.

Though the years took their toll on William, he didn't give up on his evangelical calling. He was an official delegate to the 1943 Council of the Christian Ministerial Alliance in New York City. In 1944, he spoke at the General Council in Cleveland. This was his last public appearance. William MacArthur died November 10, 1945 at the age of eighty-eight.

With the fine example of their parents, all of the MacArthur children did well in life. Only once did tragedy strike. As the story goes, the children were out hunting chestnuts in the countryside. They stopped by the farm of a Robert Ferguson, an Alliance member. The boys spied a musket on the parlor wall and took it down to play with it. An old show piece that Ferguson thought was unloaded proved itself lethal. When Alfred playfully pointed the gun at his five-year-old brother and pulled the trigger, the discharge blew away half of Roderick's head. Margaret, in a panic, covered her little brother with her dress, then they loaded Roderick into a sled. On the return trip home, Margaret clung to her dying brother the whole way. Roderick was greatly mourned, but, otherwise, the family survived and flourished.

Of particular interest is Charles Gordon MacArthur, the sixth child born to William and Georgiana on November 5, 1895. When he was 16-years-old, Charles and his 14-year-old brother were sent to Wilson Memorial Academy in Nyack, New York, to be educated. It seems, however, the educational program set up for the two boys was short-lived. Charles dropped out to take care of his mother whose illness was worsening. John, it seems, dropped out of school in the eighth grade. With that sparse educational background, John decided to try his hand as an insurance salesman; he went to work for his eldest brother Alfred's insurance company in Chicago, and John discovered his calling.

At 19-years-old, John sold one million dollars in insurance in one year. He was the top salesman, so good, in fact, the relations between Alfred and John became strained. Alfred claimed that his brother's sales methods were inappropriate, since John promised more than policies actually offered.

When World War I broke out, John enlisted in the Navy. But the discipline proved too much for him. He went AWOL, departing Chicago for Canada, where he joined the Royal Flying Corps and became a pilot, until he was involved in an airplane crash and dislocated his back.

During his convalescence in Toronto, John grew restless, and he boarded a troop train for New York. There he was discovered by the Navy who turned him over to the powers that be. Fortunately, for John, he had dated a reporter the night before his departure. She wrote a sensational news story about this patriotic young man who was so eager to fight for freedom that he'd returned to New York in an effort to serve again, despite the problems with his back.

Suddenly, John was a hero instead of a delinquent. He received a discharge from the U.S. Navy, which declared him unfit for military service, and an honorable discharge from the Royal Flying Corps. Only John D. MacArthur could pull off something like that. However, I did hear someone say once, "If there was trouble anywhere in the world, John MacArthur would be right smack dab in the middle of it all!"

As time went on, John was comforted by his success as an insurance salesman, not just in terms of income but in the assurance that he could make a mark for himself as his brothers had. Once he began to establish himself, he sought out Louise Ingals, a beautiful young woman he had met before the war. Louise was everything John wasn't — cultured, rich, sensitive and delicate. John felt that Louise would make the perfect addition to his life. Louise, in turn, admired John's vision and was certain that he would match the successes of his brothers. However, after one short year the differences between them were evident. Louise wanted a home and a family, a serene life. Though John had rented a house in the suburbs for Louise, he spent nearly all of his waking hours selling insurance. Louise seldom saw him. The marriage was disintegrating, though Louise was determined to hold the marriage together. John, however, was just as determined that his marriage not interfere with business.

John's desire to succeed was enormous. He figured to show his brother Alfred; Alfred, he thought, was a stuffed shirt who didn't know how to run an insurance company. More than anything else, he wanted to prove to Alfred that, like cream, he could "rise to the top" and become rich in his own right. Meanwhile, the president of National Life was taking note of John's outstanding sales record and dedication. He promoted John to head of the company's San Francisco office. This was John's first managerial position and a great coup. Under John's direction the San Francisco office achieved top-ranking in sales. But after just two years, John became disgruntled once again.

San Francisco seemed like the edge of the earth to John. He was convinced that Chicago was where the action was. He promptly put a man in charge of the San Francisco office, wrote the president of National Life, packed up his family and hurried back to Chicago where he was able to talk his way into a management spot with the firm. By then, John and Louise had two children, John Roderick and Virginia. But John's interest in his family waned as he became more interested in his work.

It is my personal belief that if Mr. MacArthur were here today, and I was able to ask him about his children, he would say one of two things — "It's none of your business" or "I don't believe I should have had children; I had no time for them; I was just too busy." However, I did learn over the years, though he opposed the idea from the start, he did pay for Roderick's college education. You see, Mr. MacArthur believed that every person should work like he did to make a mark in life without the luxury of formal education.

Meanwhile, John was determined to become his own boss. The opportunity presented itself when a local gas station came onto the market. John bought and hired someone to run it, and divided his attention between his new enterprise and insurance sales. The gas station soon failed; likewise his marriage. Later John said of his marriage, "My in-laws thought I was a drunkard and didn't like the late hours I was keeping selling insurance."

Next, John became interested in Alfred's young secretary, Catherine Hyland. Catherine was an attractive dark-haired young woman with a Roman Catholic upbringing. She was quiet, proper and witty with an infectious laugh and a good sense of humor. Her parents, James Hyland and Anne Nolan Hyland, had come to Chicago from Ireland. They had raised nine children, six girls and three boys.

Catherine was only an attractive teenager when she worked for National Life. In fact, this was her first job. But she was intelligent, able and very confident — a competent administrator and secretary. Meanwhile, John was still struggling to become his own boss. Then, Catherine caught his eye; obviously he had to make something of himself to prove his worth in the eyes of Catherine.

John sank his savings into a bakery. It was another losing proposition. He returned to the insurance business full time, since that was obviously where he belonged. However, he found working with his brother impossible. John quit and immediately landed another insurance sales job with a small firm, State Life Insurance Company.

With the future well in hand, Catherine quit her job, and she and John traveled to Mexico in 1916 where John obtained a divorce and married Catherine. Though such divorces and marriages were questionable, it was the best John could do, given Louise's opposition to the divorce. But he knew that Catherine was right for him — born to be his. Catherine shared his ambition, had confidence in him, and she understood his compulsive work habits. She found a new job to supplement their income. Both were dedicated to John's success in business.

As time passed, John received the opportunity he had been waiting for through a friend, Leo Lehane, an accountant in his brother Alfred's firm. Lehane discovered a small, financially shaky insurance company, Marquette Life of Jerseyville, Illinois, and it was for sale for $7,500.

John jumped at the chance to buy the company. With his managerial skills, experience and drive to succeed, he was confident he could turn the company around. Since Catherine was committed to his success and also had insurance experience, they decided to run the company together and hire additional salespeople.

In a little over a year, John and Catherine had Marquette on nearly solid footing. Then came the crash of 1929. People were cashing in insurance policies, not buying them. Further, companies with more resources than Marquette were going down the drain. John faced yet another business failure. Almost worse than financial defeat was the humiliation before his brothers. However, with the help of his friend Leo Lehane, John and Catherine managed to keep Marquette afloat during the depression years.

Of all of William's children, only John dispensed with religion altogether. Yet, as a reflection of his parents' training, he used Biblical allusions and quotations throughout his life. Nevertheless, he had little regard for the conventions of society and was described by journalist Stewart Alsop as a "born nose thumper". John took great satisfaction in puncturing the egos of those who annoyed him or stood in his way. But in spite of this deliberately tough exterior, John had a sentimental side, though he would not admit it. Those who knew him well attested to his warmth and sense of humor, qualities he claimed to have absorbed from his dear sweet mother.

Finally, the breakthrough John had hoped for came in 1935. A state insurance examiner John knew stopped by the Marquette office and casually mentioned that Bankers Life and Casualty Company was in trouble. It had a $2,500 debt it could not meet. However, the examiner said the company was sound, ten years old but poorly managed.

Immediately, John inquired at the State Attorney General's office about buying the company. He learned that he could do it, if he paid the company's debt that day.

All of John's cash was tied up in his business. But not to be deterred, he borrowed the money from two friends and one of them was the faithful Leo Lehane. This was the beginning of the long road to success for John D. and Catherine T. MacArthur.

By 1947, Bankers Life and Casualty had expanded into fourteen states and had a premium income of $5.5 million. And success begot success. No matter the field of endeavor, John succeeded.

What kept him going?

Said MacArthur: "I had declared that I was going to build a company. I was so committed to that that I actually thought,

I actually believed, that if I failed, I would never get another job in the insurance industry. They would say, 'Get him outta here.' So I stayed with it."

When he was a millionaire many times over, John ignored conspicuous consumption. He was deeply contemptuous of the idle rich. For all his success, John remained somewhat insecure, though. I think something that his son Roderick once said is indicative of this insecurity. Roderick recalled a conversation he had with his father in 1946:

"The first time my father ever talked to me about having money beyond the immediate edge of struggling was when I was 25-years-old. I came to visit him, and we sat on a boat in Fort Lauderdale, and he explained that finally, finally, I should understand that he was really over the hump, that in a very short time, he would be worth maybe as much as $10 million. Good old Dad, he always dreamed that some day he would be over the hump. Well, dream on."

In 1948, John's and Catherine's marriage began to fall apart. Catherine left John and went to live with her sister Patricia. John sought reconciliation, but Catherine refused to speak with him. John then went to see Patricia in her office at Alfred's firm and pleaded with her to influence Catherine to return.

Patricia responded, "I can't do anything about it. She has a mind of her own."

Then, the fun started. Catherine sued John for $2.5 million, claiming half the worth of Bakers Life as his business partner. John counter-sued for desertion. Unable to work out a settlement, MacArthur found himself in court during the summer of 1949, facing not a business foe but his wife.

After four long hours of arguments by lawyers on both sides, the Chicago Circuit Court Judge Harry M. Fisher, who was hearing the case, said, "I want to see you, here" he pointed to Catherine "and you, here" he pointed to John "alone in my chambers — without your lawyers."

What transpired behind closed doors is not a matter of record. But a reconciliation was affected, and Catherine returned to John's side where she obviously belonged.

In subsequent years, the MacArthur businesses expanded tremendously. And 1958 saw John and Catherine spending most of their time in Florida where his real estate interests were growing. In fact, he was already at work building his "dream city" of Palm Beach Gardens, an attractive adjunct to West Palm Beach to this day. Meantime, Bankers Life had grown into a billion dollar enterprise. But the insurance company was only part of the fortune being amassed. John had become, not only the richest member of his family but the wealthiest man in the nation.

As for his brother Charles — now a Pulitzer Prize-winning playwright — alcoholism had caught up with him. His wife Helen Hayes, the renowned actress, stayed at his side, whispering at the end, "I love you, Charlie."

In the true MacArthur Clan spirit, Charles winked at her and said, "You should."

On the morning of April 21, 1956, Charles MacArthur died. He was buried in Oak Hill Cemetery in Nyack, New York.

John D. MacArthur died on January 6, 1978 at Good Samaritan Hospital, West Palm Beach, Florida, from pancreatic cancer. His wife Catherine survived him by almost four years, dying in her apartment on December 15, 1981, after a long battle with cancer.

Catherine's will left a large part of her estate to charity with over $3 million each going to local charities — St. Mary's Hospital, Good Samaritan Hospital Hospice and the Animal Rescue League of the Palm Beaches. She also willed over $12 million to Palm Beach Atlantic College.

The last surviving child of William and Georgiana MacArthur was their eldest daughter Marguerite MacArthur Wiley. An unassuming and kindly woman, she lived quietly with her daughter Lois in St. Charles, Illinois, and remained active in the church. She died on June 15, 1986 at the age of 99 in Delnor Community Hospital in St. Charles.

Actress Helen Hayes, Charles' wife, died on March 17, 1992 of heart failure in Nyack, New York. She was 92 years old.

John Roderick MacArthur, the only son of billionaire John D. MacArthur, attended Rollins College in Florida. He traveled in Mexico during the 1940s where he was a sometimes reporter for the Associated Press. During World War II, he joined the Civilian Ambulance Corps, American Field Service. He participated in the Allied invasion of France and later served with the French Underground Resistance Union.

Later Roderick built a business of his own, an international market for limited edition collector plates — such as commemorative Christmas plates. The business enterprise became what we now know as the Bradford Exchange.

Although Roderick and his father had strained relations for many years, they did have a reconciliation at the Colonnades Beach Hotel just before MacArthur's death. From behind the bar at the Colonnades, I witnessed this wonderful embrace between father and son. The memory of this reconciliation has stayed with me to this day — close to my heart.

After his father's death, Roderick became closely allied with the John D. and Catherine T. MacArthur Foundation. He also purchased the Holiday Inn on PGA Boulevard in Palm Beach Gardens, Florida, and expanded it into a much larger hotel with a five-star restaurant.

J. Roderick MacArthur died of the same illness as his father at the age of 63 on December 15, 1984. He was survived by his wife, the former Christine Lentendart, his two sons, Gregory and John "Rick" Roderick MacArthur, and daughter Solange, and his sister Virginia de Cordova, two nephews and a niece.

Virginia de Cordova, Roderick's sister, is the lone surviving child of John D. MacArthur and his first wife. John and Catherine had no children. Virginia married a university professor who taught in Mexico City, and this is where they currently reside.

Having had this brief review of the MacArthur family, and in particular John D. MacArthur, let's now look at the John D. MacArthur for whom I worked — the man his employees called, "The Skipper."

Chapter 3

The Interview

For me, the beginning was 1975. I was working as beverage manager for the Red Carpet Inn, Tampa, Florida. Things were pretty good there; I'd made a name for myself. In fact, I had done a good deal of promotional work for the hotel and put the lounge on its feet. Unfortunately, the hotel had a multitude of problems; financially it wasn't doing well. So, as the days went by, I watched the management team come in and cut all of the promotions I'd started — which were working; and I realized the future held little promise. I decided to quit my job. In other words, I saw the handwriting on the wall and gave two weeks' notice.

I figured I'd best look for a new job. In the interim, I received a phone call from a friend. The fellow's name was Dale; he had worked as a sales director with me and helped on the promotions at the Red Carpet Inn. During his travels, he'd ended up at the Colonnades Beach Hotel on the east coast of Florida and been interviewed for the job of general manager. However, he understood there was quite a history of general managers connected with the hotel and decided not to take the job. But he mentioned to me in passing that the owner, John D. MacArthur, was in need of a beverage manager, someone who could straighten out his beverage department; it was, according to Dale, in complete chaos.

Dale suggested he set up an interview for me with MacArthur. "Maybe we've got something here for you."

"That's fine," I told him. "Let's do it!" I thanked him and agreed to wait for his call. I didn't have long to wait.

The next day Dale phoned and said, "Bob, I've got the interview all set up. Mr. MacArthur is very interested in talking to you. I think, if everything goes well, you'll have yourself a job over here — if you want it."

In passing, he mentioned to me that MacArthur was the second richest man in the United States (Daniel K. Ludwig, a shipping tycoon, was first), and that the hotel was located directly on the ocean at Palm Beach Shores, Florida.

All of this sounded marvelous to me. Thanking him again, I assured him I would go to work making arrangements to get over there.

I was so excited with the prospects, I could hardly contain myself.

My wife said, "Go for it. What have you got to lose?"

She was right, of course. Even if I didn't get the job, I'd meet MacArthur and see the sights. It was worth the trip alone for that kind of opportunity.

I picked up the phone and called the hotel. I arranged to meet Mr. MacArthur at nine o'clock on the morning of August 15th.

Needless to say, I arrived at the hotel ahead of time, eight o'clock that morning. Dale was still registered there, so I phoned his room. Dale said, "I'll meet you in the lobby in five minutes."

When he arrived he asked, "Do you see that little table in the corner over there at the coffee shop entrance? That's where you're going to have your interview."

**John D. MacArthur at his office —
a table in the coffee shop of the
Colonnades Beach Hotel (1976).**

Permission: John D. and Catherine T.
MacArthur Foundation, Chicago, IL.

I stared at the table; a man was sitting there. "Who's that at the table."

"Don't be alarmed. That's Mr. MacArthur."

For a second or so, I contemplated the man. Though I understood he was 77-years-old, he looked like a pretty healthy man for his age. However, his overall appearance was unkempt. His clothing looked to me as if they might have been purchased at a fire sale. If he had stood up straight — which I never saw him do in the years I worked for him — he would have been at least six feet tall. But he walked in a slightly bent-over fashion, sporting a rather noticeable paunch. As for his hair, what there was of it, it appeared that he paid little attention to it. He also had a moustache that seemed hardly worth the effort.

Since Dale had already had an interview with MacArthur, he gave me a couple of good tips. "When you sit down at the table, do a lot of listening and very little talking. Mr. MacArthur is a good judge of personal character. He'll be talking to you about lots of different things — some of them seemingly unimportant — then, all of a sudden he'll fire a business question at you just to see how you respond. If the interview goes well, and you and Mr. MacArthur start talking about salary, make sure you shoot as high as you can. From what I've heard about this hotel, once you make a deal with him on money, it's possible you won't ever get more."

I nodded and said, "Wish me luck!"

He did.

And I went off to meet John D. MacArthur, the second richest man in the U.S.

Walking up to his table, I said, "Mr. MacArthur? I believe I have an appointment with you this morning. My name is Bob Sanford."

Mr. MacArthur looked up, his crystalline blue eyes, sparkling. "Young man, please have a seat."

I sat down across the table from him; I couldn't believe this was the man that was interviewing me for a job. The second richest man in the country? He didn't look like a rich man at all. In fact, he looked like he didn't have two nickels to rub together.

Wrinkled slacks, a dingy once-white shirt, an old sweater was what he wore; and I assumed, from all the evidence, that this little table was his office. I had imagined being interviewed in some big, fancy office with carpet sinking deep around my ankles. What next?

Mr. MacArthur started by asking me, "Why did you leave your last job? Have you ever been in this area of Florida before?"

I answered those questions as well as other questions, many of which I'm sure he already knew the answers. But never mind. I did my best.

After about fifteen minutes, he stood up and said, "Bob, let's go outside." He pointed toward the door that led outside the coffee shop. "Why don't you go and sit on that step out there? I'll be right out."

I went out to the step and sat down. Shortly, I looked over my shoulder to see Mr. MacArthur coming from the kitchen with a great big trash barrel. He was wheeling it across the floor. I just sat there and stared in disbelief.

Finally, the door opened and the trash barrel came flying through the door to be plopped down right in front of me. Then, he sat on the step beside me and began throwing food from the barrel into the air, his face breaking into a big grin as ducks came squawking from everywhere.

"Bob," said MacArthur, "do you mind helping me?"

Why not? I thought. I reached into the trash barrel and started throwing food to the ducks, my hands covered with

God-knows-what-all. I'd had some odd interviews in my day, but this was the strangest of all.

MacArthur looked at me, his blue eyes a-twinkle and said, "I bet you think I'm nuts — "

"Mr. MacArthur," I said, calling upon all the resolution I possessed, "I don't think you're nuts."

"Good. That's a goddamn good answer. Because I have two reasons for doing this. Number one: I love my ducks. Bob, you take a good look at that trash barrel. You see that half a loaf of bread?"

I nodded.

"Take it out and look it all over."

I removed the bread from the trash barrel.

"Now, do you see anything wrong with that loaf of bread?"

"No, sir," I said. "I don't see anything wrong with it."

"Do you see any reason why anybody couldn't eat it?"

I examined the bread carefully. "No."

"Well, that's the second reason I do this. Just look at all the waste that's going on in my kitchen."

We fed the ducks a bit longer, then MacArthur said, "Well, that's going to do it. The ducks are fed. Let's go back inside."

We stepped inside, where I found a napkin to wipe my hands. I stood there in amazement, while MacArthur wrestled the trash barrel back into the kitchen. I could hear him yelling and screaming in the kitchen about the terrible waste of food . . .

I thought to myself: This probably goes on every single day; he feeds his ducks, goes in the kitchen, yells at the chef about waste. It probably makes him feel good. As for the waste of food, it probably made little difference!

Finally, Mr. MacArthur came back and sat at the table. I had brought along a brief case full of promotional material I'd done in the past, mainly for the Red Carpet Inn. I thought

Mr. Mac feeding his beloved ducks.

Permission: *The Palm Beach Post,*
Photographer, John J. Lopinot.

he might be interested. I spread the papers out on the table.

MacArthur looked them over and seemed to like what he saw, saying, from time to time, "Oh, boy, that's nice! When did you do that?"

Of course, I had all the answers.

We talked a little while more. I pushed the materials back into the brief case. Then, he glanced at his watch and said, "Okay. That's it. It's four o'clock. That will do it for to-day." He picked up the phone and said, "Please send Mr. K over to the table."

In a couple of minutes, a handsome, young man in his twenties with dark brown hair, brown eyes — a classy dresser — in a white shirt, tie and suit appeared before us.

"This is Bob Sanford," MacArthur said. He'll be spending the night here in the hotel. Fix him up with a nice room. I want to see him at nine o'clock sharp in the morning."

Said I, "Thank you very much, Mr. MacArthur. See you in the morning."

At that, MacArthur excused himself, and Mr. K and I walked toward the lobby, Mr. K saying to me, "Well, how did it go?"

I sighed. "I really don't know."

"What do you mean by that?"

"Well," I said, "it was an interesting interview. But he didn't tell me whether I had a job or not."

Mr. K accompanied me into the elevator and showed me to my room. My room turned out to be a suite. What a surprise!

"This is the Paul Harvey Suite," Mr. K explained.

I wasn't too sure in those days who Paul Harvey was. I had no idea he was an influential radio commentator out of Chicago and a longtime friend of MacArthur. But that was okay. I was impressed by the generosity of the suite.

Mr. K. went his way, and I set about straightening things out in my room. I couldn't help wondering who this Mr. K. might be. I assumed he must be the general manager. But Mr. MacArthur didn't introduce him as such. I shrugged my shoulders and thought about the interview. I was totally at sea.

About a half hour later, I decided to take a trip down to the cocktail lounge, look it over and see what was going on there. As I approached the lounge area, I noticed it was really quite different from anything I had ever seen before.

It was a straight bar — 40 feet long. Behind the bar, indirect black lighting was shining on a mural. I studied the effect for a few minutes, trying to make sense of it. Giving up, I walked past the bar, and in between the dining room and the bar, there was a carousel with tables and chairs. A piano player was tinkling the ivories in the middle, and the carousel was revolving. I sat down on the carousel and looked the lounge over.

Behind the bar was a sloppily dressed barmaid with a cigarette hanging from the corner of her mouth. Pretty depressing. A cocktail waitress — a fetching young girl — stood by the service bar. I beckoned her over and ordered a drink.

When she brought my drink she sat down next to me, saying quietly, " I'm Mary. How did it go today?"

Playing it dumb, I asked, "What do you mean?"

"I understand you had an interview with Mr. MacArthur." Mary had a very nice smile; it seemed to brighten the moment and take away doubt.

"Yeah, I did. I guess the word's out on that," I said, feeling somewhat better.

"Oh," she said, "it's never a secret when Mr. MacArthur has an interview, especially if it's someone who might be coming into the hotel."

We made some small talk, then she asked, "Well, how

did he leave it with you?"

"He said he'd see me in the morning."

She thought about that for a minute and smiled encouragement. "You know, I've been here a little while. I've seen many interviews take place at that table over there. I can tell you one thing. You spent most of the day with him, and he said he wanted to see you tomorrow. That's a good sign. There's one thing I do know about John D. MacArthur. He doesn't spend much time talking to people he's not interested in."

Feeling a bit more hopeful, my mind less clouded with doubt, I introduced myself.

Mary was an eye-catching girl, I must admit, and not because of her physical beauty. She had a smile that could put anyone in a good mood instantly. Though soft-spoken, I found her interesting to talk to. True enough, she was only in her twenties. She did have long blonde hair that fell well below her shoulders and seemed to sway with every movement, but she was not flirtatious. In fact, her attitude and gestures were refined. In my opinion, she was a genuine girl and a real asset to the lounge.

I told Mary how nice it was to meet her. I said, "If everything goes well tomorrow morning, maybe we'll be working together." Then, I wished her a good evening and got up from the carousel. As I did so, I was attracted to the main dining room. I had never seen anything quite so beautiful — big crystal chandeliers hanging from the ceiling; crisp white linens on the tables; all the staff dressed in tuxedos. Beyond the far front of the dining room through the large glass windows waterfalls with colored lights were reflected; the lawn with the ocean lay just beyond. It was a magnificent and impressive sight to behold — real class.

Having rubbed shoulders with the upper-crust of the world, I felt in need of a good night's sleep. But it didn't come easily. I kept going back to my interview, over and over in my mind. I couldn't help wondering what tomorrow might bring.

Not much had changed from the day before. Mr. MacArthur was sitting at the same table, dressed in the same clothes, a cigarette hanging from his mouth, sipping a cup of black coffee.

I sat down across from him, and we talked for about an hour. Then, he said, "Bob, let's go for a walk. I want to take you on a tour of my property."

So, off we went, and it was more than a tour; It was a very long hike. Since it was August, it was hot as hinges out there. I wished for a thermos of ice water to see me through the ordeal.

MacArthur took me down to the Paradise Building at the far south end of the property. We went through the over-sized glass doors on the ground floor into a spacious ball-room. Here I noticed those huge crystal chandeliers again overhead. This room had a full stage. MacArthur said that many times over the years he'd had big-name entertainment on stage. In fact, the room was used for large gatherings of up to 800 people. He then directed me through the kitchen area.

My heart sank. The kitchen looked to be dysfunctional in the truest sense of the word. In fact, the kitchen was terribly run down, as if nothing there might be in working order.

We then proceeded out the front door of the Paradise Building and made our way to the main building, past all the little shops and boutiques — a barbershop, a store that sold out-of-town newspapers, cigarettes, cigars, a fashion boutique for women. At the end of the shops, Mr. MacArthur took me down a little breezeway called Streets of Paris. It was unique with its wrought iron tables and chairs outside, and murals covering the walls. It was a nice place to sit and have lunch on a pleasant day.

Next we took in the tiki bar on the beach; it was glassed in with a thatched roof. I was shown all around the bar, and I marveled aloud at how nice it was.

Now we doubled back on the left side of the main building; there a beautiful Olympic-sized saltwater swimming pool with a bar and cabanas all around it awaited us. I was impressed and said as much.

"Wait until you see the Andros Building," said MacArthur.

And off we went across the lawn on the back side of the property to the newest addition. The Andros Building held a health spa on the ground floor. Around back was another swimming pool, not as large as the one we'd just seen. But many rooms for guests encircled it.

By now, I was beginning to realize what a vast piece of property this was. "This is something else again," I said.

MacArthur glanced at me, eyes twinkling. "Well, I think it's time to go back to the office for a cup of coffee."

I must say that I was a bit relieved, impressed though I was. Boy, was it hot out there!

As we returned to the coffee shop, we encountered ducks all over the lawn. They were everywhere. Just everywhere — a population explosion, I should think. Whatever, once we were back inside the coffee shop, we sat down at Mr. MacArthur's office table.

Now he looked me squarely in the eyes and said, "Bob, what do you really think of my property?"

I thought that one over carefully, remembering this was still a job interview. "Well, Mr. MacArthur," I said, "to be honest with you, I think you have a beautiful piece of property here. But it does need work."

He snorted. "Bob, if you were going to be honest with me, you'd tell me that this place is a goddamn dump."

Streets of Paris at Colonnades Beach Hotel.

Permission: Bobbie Lemay (1984).

I straightened my shoulders, trying for the proper response. "I don't think I should tell you that. After all, I'm over here for a job interview."

"Oh, I see. Well, I'll accept the fact then that it needs work."

With that, we were off and flying on another wide ranging conversation. I hadn't mentioned that I had to be back in Tampa at seven o'clock that night. My ex-employees and friends were having a going-away party for me. I didn't want to miss it. After awhile I decided I ought to mention the fact; and I did.

"Oh, boy!" he said; then, he paused. "Well, Bob, I guess it's time we talk a little *beezneessss.*" And he got right to the point. "You do realize that this is going to be a big job. I'm going to need somebody to take over this whole beverage department."

"Yes, sir, I realize that. I was told that upfront."

"What kind of money do you think you'd need?"

I forget now what I told him.

But he seemed to think the salary I mentioned was okay. "Fair enough," he said.

I decided to prompt him now. "How do you want to work this?"

"Well, why don't we do this? I understand you have a mobile home in Tampa. I was told that your wife is working there. Why don't you let your wife and your mobile home stay right there. You and I will work on a 30 day trial basis. In other words, you fly over here. You go right to work, and we'll see how it goes. If everything goes well, you like me and I like you, that's fine. If not, no harm done."

I shook his hand, saying, "That sounds pretty fair to me, Mr. MacArthur."

He started to walk away.

"Excuse me, sir, when do you want me to report over here?"

He turned and said, "I don't give a damn when you report. But when you do, you goddamn sure better be ready to work."

Said I, "If it takes me seven days a week, 15 hours a day, I'll straighten out your beverage department. You can bet your life on it."

"Good," he said. "See you then."

On the plane trip back to Tampa, I reflected on my interview with MacArthur. My only regret was that I had made one mistake during the interview. At one point, feeling on top of things, I had called him, "John," followed swiftly by a profuse apology.

"Look, Bob, don't ever call me — John. Call me, Mr. MacArthur. Call me, Mr. Mac. But don't ever call me — John. Even my friends don't call me that. I don't have any of those, you know."

I apologized again, saying, "It was just a slip, and it won't happen again." And I made myself a promise that it would never happen again and hoped for the best.

Little did I imagine, I was in for the ride of my life.

Chapter 4

Thirty Long Days

Mr. K greeted me upon my return to the hotel. "Mr. MacArthur is waiting for you. I'll tell him you're here."

This Mr. K was a true fashion plate. He looked like a million dollars himself. What with being well over six feet tall and lithe in form, he cut quite a figure. But I didn't put him down for it. He was a hands-on kind of guy, I sensed, the kind of person who could take control and do it just right — whatever it might be.

When Mr. K returned, he said, "Mr. MacArthur wants to talk with you at his table."

I nodded and hurried off to the coffee shop, where I found MacArthur waiting. It was as if no time had passed at all, since I'd seen him last. He was wearing the same clothes, the coffee was black and a cigarette hung from the corner of his mouth.

He greeted me with the words, "Welcome aboard, Bob. Are you ready for some hard work?"

"Ready as I'll ever be." I was rarin' to go.

"Good! Then, let's get started."

He took me around the lounge area and showed me how it was set up. Then, he called Mr. K over and told him to give me the key to the liquor room. That done, he gave Mr. K instructions regarding my lodging. "We'll give Bob an apartment across the street from the hotel, since he'll be in the hotel most of the time anyway. We don't want him to get too far away."

Once I settled into my new apartment, I rushed over to the hotel and got busy. It didn't take me long to figure out that I would be replacing two people, perhaps three.

Mr. MacArthur had people set up temporarily, until he could find someone to reorganize the whole beverage department. He had the barmaid that I'd seen earlier, he had a guy doing all the ordering — liquor, beer, etc. — and he had a man who would come in just in the morning to straighten the bar from the previous evening and get it ready to open at four o'clock in the afternoon.

I thought to myself, What a waste!

After a brief conversation with the man who was doing the ordering, it was amazing to me that the hotel received anything. He had no records — just telephone numbers. It was obvious he had no idea what he was doing. Mary was the only waitress. I telephoned her and asked her to come to the hotel.

Mary came right over, arriving with the words, "I'm sure glad you got the job. Maybe things'll get done right around here for a change."

I sat Mary down on the carousel and asked her many policy questions. As it turned out, there was no policy at all on anything. For instance, "When does the barmaid usually arrive?"

"That varies. But she's supposed to be here at four o'clock."

"What time do you start?" I asked.

"Four-thirty."

To familiarize myself with the operation, I had a good look in the liquor room, checked the supply room and generally cased my territory. Now was the time to talk with Mr. MacArthur again, I decided.

MacArthur was sitting at his table alone. When I appeared before him, he said, "How's it going?"

"So far, so good. I can see we've a lot of work to do."

"Yep." He nodded. "We sure do. You can handle it."

The first thing I wanted to talk to him about was the unsightly barmaid who came in when it pleased her. I cleared my throat and got to the gist of it, then asked him when he wanted me to go behind the bar.

"Well, Bob, to be honest with you, that girl is kinda doing me a favor. She's not making any money here, since it's pretty slow this time of year. As you can see, some of these people I just kept on — until I could get you in here."

Ah, I thought . . .

MacArthur added, "I'll tell you what. Why don't we do this? Why don't you come in this afternoon at four o'clock. She should be here by then. Simply tell her that you're going to be working with her for the evening. See how that goes."

"Okay," I said. "I'll do just that."

I excused myself and went back to work. I knew what he was doing. He was setting me up to get rid of the barmaid. I also knew this was only the beginning of the changes I would have to make.

At four o'clock sharp, I walked behind the bar. Miracle of miracles, the barmaid was there, getting things set up. Everybody called her, Whacka. But that seemed so unreal, I decided I'd try the conventional route of learning her real name. I said to her, "I'm Bob Sanford. I'm going to be working with you tonight."

"You're going to be working with me?" she sneered.

"Bullshit! If you're working behind the bar, I'm outta here."
She slammed the keys down on the bar and out the door she
went as fast as her legs could carry her.

Well, she had read my mind and had saved me the trouble
of dismissing her. Personally, I felt badly about how it had
happened, but I also knew she had to go. There was no other
way.

At about 4:30, MacArthur came in and sat at the bar.

I placed a cocktail napkin in front of him, as if he might
be a customer.

"Uh-oh, no, no, no. You don't give me a cocktail napkin —
ever."

"Right," I said and quickly removed the napkin, obviously a wasteful gesture. "What would you like, sir?"

He pointed to a bottle, marked: MacArthur Scotch. "See
that bottle there? That's all you ever give me. Don't ever give
me anything else. That's my own scotch. I had it made up
especially for me. That's all I ever drink."

When I served the scotch I placed a stir stick in his drink.

He took it out and threw it on the bar. "That's another
thing you've got to learn, Bob. Don't ever give me one of those,
either. Nothing but a waste of money."

"I guess you're right, Mr. MacArthur. A terrible waste of
money." Then, I mentioned the barmaid incident to him.

"Gee, Bob, I'm sorry about that," he said smoothly, a
twinkle in his eyes. "Maybe I should have taken care of that
myself. But it was bound to happen — sooner or later."

I simply said, "I'm sure you're right about that one, Mr.
MacArthur."

Now he said, "Bob, if anybody comes up to this bar, and
they tell you not to bother making out a check for them, you
put that check in front of them instantly. They may tell you
that they're friends of mine. But I don't have any friends. I

don't want any friends. And I didn't get rich by having friends."

I knew he had a good reason for telling me that; and it wasn't too long before I had figured out how to handle the situation.

About an hour after MacArthur departed the bar, sure enough, a fellow came in, sat down and said, "You're new around here, ain't ya?"

"Yes, I am brand spankin' new."

"How long do you think you're going to be around?"

"No idea."

He ordered a drink. But when I went to make out the check, he said, "Oh, you don't have to do that. Me and Mr. MacArthur are good friends. They don't ever make checks out for me."

Quick on the draw, I responded, "I'll tell you what we're going to do. You probably are a very good friend of Mr. MacArthur. I have to believe that's true. However, being a new bartender, I have to protect myself. So, I'm going to put the check in front of you, and if Mr. MacArthur should come by and pick it up, that's all well and good."

MacArthur never did come by and pick up the check. Reluctantly, the customer paid.

That first evening I kept pretty much to myself, reorganizing things. I closed the bar at one o'clock in the morning and walked across the street to my apartment. I returned to the bar the next morning at eight o'clock sharp.

While setting up the bar for the new shift, I heard that the barmaid, who'd rushed off in such a huff, had just come out of the hospital. I thought, Oh, my God. What happened to her?

It turned out that she'd gotten so upset with me, she'd taken a bunch of pills and had had to go to the hospital to have her stomach pumped out. I felt awful. I had never imagined she'd take it that hard. Then, again, perhaps that's why they called her — Whacka . . . Here, though, the plot started to thicken.

It seemed she was hired by one of Mr. MacArthur's personal bodyguards. The bodyguard ran a local karate school and hung around with a very mean crowd. Of course, he blamed me for the whole incident. In fact, in time, I found out a plot had been concocted by this bunch of characters to get rid of me. I suspect that if I hadn't been hired by MacArthur himself, I'd not be telling this story. Their reputation around town was something to behold.

After a couple of days on the job, I decided it was time to reorganize the staff. The first person to go was the fellow who did the ordering. I planned to do all the ordering and inventory myself. The second to go was the fellow who came in to clean up the bar in the morning; I would be doing his job too. This made for a long day, but I didn't mind it. The additional chores kept me busy and in control of the situation.

I was given a little office in back — among many other little offices — where I had a desk, telephone and lots of paperwork. The Colonnades handled a large number of parties and functions. All of those function sheets, of course, ended up on my desk.

Basically, the first thing in the morning, I went into my office and did paperwork. Then, I hurried out to the bar and straightened everything up for the four o'clock opening. Around noon, I'd leave the hotel and return at 3:30 in the afternoon, so that I might open the bar at four o'clock sharp.

The only employee that I hung on to was Mary. She was a good waitress, she lived close by, and she knew all of the people.

When I first found out that I'd be taking the job at the

Apéritifs and Dessert Wines

	Glass
DUBONNET RED or BLOND	1.25
STOCK VERMOUTH (Sweet or Dry)	.75
CHERRY KIJAFA, Denmark	.85
BLACKBERRY JULEP, Italy	.85
SOLERA CREAM SHERRY, GREAT WESTERN	.85

Red Wines

Bin No.		½ Bottle	Bottle
1	MOUTON CADET, Baron Philippe de Rothschild *From the great chateau of Mouton Rothschild*	3.75	7.00
2	BEAUJOLAIS ST. LOUIS, Barton & Guestier, Vintage *Delicate and fruity*	3.75	6.50
3	POMMARD, Barton & Guestier, Vintage *Full bodied, firm and lovely*	7.00	13.00
4	CHATEAUNEUF DU PAPE, Barton & Guestier, Vintage *Full bodied and luscious*	4.75	9.00
5	CABERNET SAUVIGNON, Paul Masson, California *Velvety smooth - exquisite character*	3.25	5.50
6	BACO NOIR, BURGUNDY, GREAT WESTERN, N. Y. State *Hearty and well-balanced*	2.50	4.50

Rosé Wines

Bin No.		½ Bottle	Bottle
7	NECTAROSE, VIN ROSÉ, France *Medium dry, very delightful*	3.00	5.25
8	LANCERS, Portugal *Light and dry*	4.50	8.50
9	ROSÉ, GREAT WESTERN, N. Y. State *Fresh and fragrant*	2.50	4.50

White Wines

Bin No.		½ Bottle	Bottle
10	MOUTON CADET, Baron Philippe de Rothschild *From the great chateau of Mouton Rothschild*	3.75	7.00
11	CHABLIS, Barton & Guestier, Vintage *Very fine, elegant and dry*	4.25	8.00
12	POUILLY FUISSÉ, Barton & Guestier, Vintage *Very dry, vigorous and steely*	4.75	9.0
13	LIEBFRAUMILCH GLOCKENSPIEL, Julius Kayser, Vintage *Full bodied, fruity and dry*		3.50
14	BERNKASTELER RIESLING, Julius Kayser, Vintage *Fruity, delicate and fresh*		3.50
15	SAUTERNE, Paul Masson, California *Light, medium dry and charming*		2.50
16	DUTCHESS RHINE, GREAT WESTERN, N. Y. State *Medium dry and delicious*	2.50	4.50

Champagnes and Sparkling Wines

Bin No.		½ Bottle	Bottle
17	MUMM'S CORDON ROUGE, BRUT, France	11.50	21.50
18	MOET & CHANDON BRUT, Vintage, France	12.50	23.50
19	DOM PERIGNON		35.00
20	GREAT WESTERN EXTRA DRY, N. Y. State	5.25	9.50
21	PAUL MASSON SPARKLING BURGUNDY, California	4.75	8.75
22	PAUL MASSON VERY COLD DUCK, California	4.75	8.75

To add to your dining pleasure may we suggest

PAUL MASSON

BURGUNDY —   ROSÉ —   CHABLIS —

Glass .85   ½ Carafe 2.75   Full Carafe 4.50

Wine List from the Colonnades Beach Hotel.

Colonnades, I'd called my dad in Cape Cod, Massachusetts, and told him the news.

Dad said, "When you get over there, look in the phone book and see if you can find Pat DiPietro. There can't be many names like that in the phone book. I'm sure he lives in that neighborhood somewhere."

At first, I was so busy I didn't give it a thought. Then, one night I was working the bar, and I heard this guy at the end of the bar. He had a gravel voice, and he was talking with the fellow next to him about Cape Cod. I hurried over to him and said, "I haven't met you. But my name is Bob Sanford."

"My name," he said, "is Pat DiPietro."

"For God's sake!" I exclaimed. "My dad told me to look you up. I've been so busy, I haven't had a chance."

We had a good chat about my dad, which proves, I think, how small the world is.

The first three weeks at the Colonnades flew by, and MacArthur hadn't said a word pro or con to me. Finally, though, during that third week, Mr. MacArthur came up to the bar and said, "Bob, come over to the carousel. I want to have a talk with you."

I sensed this was it. I was doing a good job, and I knew it. But I was jittery.

Once we were settled in, Mr. MacArthur said, "Bob, you know I'm real proud of the job you're doing. I think you're going to be a real asset to this hotel. The question is: Do you like it here? Do you want to stay?"

Inwardly, I heaved a sigh of relief. "Like it? I certainly do. I think there's much that can be done, and I've started working on that — as I hope you've already seen." Then, I mentioned my wife coming over and our mobile home that would have to be moved.

"That won't be any problem," MacArthur said. "I'll take care of that for you. You let me know when she's coming over, and I'll make arrangements to get you a lot for the mobile home. By the way, you won't have to pay any rent on that lot as long as you work for me."

I thanked him. This was a truly nice gesture; and he didn't have to do it, but he did.

I couldn't wait to call my wife. So, sometime that afternoon, I rang her up.

She was pleased and promised to get with the arrangements. Two days later she phoned and said, "Our mobile home should be over there in two days."

I spoke with Mr. MacArthur about this.

"Well, there shouldn't be any problem. Go out to Northlake Boulevard to a trailer park — Hilltop Gardens. As soon as you pull in there, you'll see an office. Go into the office and talk to a fellow named Felix. Tell Felix that your mobile home will be here in a couple of days and have him assign you a lot."

I did exactly that.

Said Felix, "Mr. MacArthur actually told you that he had a lot for you? We don't have any empty lots."

"Well, maybe you should give him a call . . . "

Felix picked up the phone and had a short conversation. When he dropped the phone back in its cradle he said, "Mr. MacArthur told me to build you a lot."

"What does that mean?"

His shoulders sagged, and he heaved a huge sigh. "I really don't know. But we'll have to get something for you. Come on, Bob. We'll ride around back in my truck and see what we can do."

At the back of the trailer park, many spaces were empty. Felix looked around frantically. "How about right here?"

he said, pointing to a vacancy.

I nodded; it looked fine to me.

"But," he added, "there's a bit of a problem."

"What's that?"

"Well, we might not be able to get electricity to you right away." Then, Felix explained that MacArthur had an on-going feud with the electric company. The water and gas company wouldn't be any problem, though, since MacArthur owned these companies.

"Well," I said, "we'll just cross that bridge when we come to it." At least, I would have a place for my mobile home. I thanked Felix for his help and returned to the hotel, once again keeping my fingers crossed.

The mobile home arrived on schedule along with my wife. However, none of this mattered too much, since I was so busy I hardly saw home or wife. Everything was moving ahead smoothly, except for the electricity at home. We had none. After a week or so, my wife began to complain, and I didn't blame her. I spoke to Mr. MacArthur about the problem.

"Oh, no electricity?" he said, as if the thought hadn't crossed his mind. "Well, don't you worry about that, Bob. I'll take care of it."

Another couple of days went by. No electricity. I hated to bother Mr. MacArthur again; I was fearful he'd think, What a pain in the ass this guy is! and sweep it all under the rug.

Still, he was the only one who could straighten out the electrical problem, and I knew it. So, I pulled myself together and approached him again.

"Hummm," he went. "No electricity, huh?" He leaned back in his chair, as if thinking.

"That's it!" he exclaimed. "By tomorrow morning, you'll have electricity. Believe me."

At about 7:30 the following morning, I looked out the

window of my mobile home to see what a commotion was all about. Two trucks with three men, clipboards in hand, were on the scene. Aw, I thought; I rushed outside to see what was going on. Could these be the men who could give us electricity? Yes and no. There was a problem.

The mobile home was situated on the lot in an unfortunate position. Half of it was in the city; half of it was in the county. Therefore, on hand was a man from the city, a man from the county and one of MacArthur's henchmen. However, they all assured me that this problem would be solved, and electricity would be flowing into the mobile home by afternoon.

I shook hands all around with great thanks, then headed for the hotel, hopeful the problem would be solved. Around 4:30 that afternoon my wife called and said, "Hooray! We have electricity!"

Such was MacArthur's clout, when he put his mind to it. But, then, Mr. MacArthur's favorite saying, as I was to learn in days ahead was "All's well that ends well," and, of course, everything had ended well!

Chapter 5

A Cast of Characters

One of the most interesting things about the Colonnades Beach Hotel was the "cast of characters", as I like to refer to them. These people were always around. The location of the bar — in the middle of everything — made it a perfect spot from which to view these characters as they came and went.

Mr. MacArthur had a line of such characters waiting to see him every day. One of the characters was our head maintenance man. I called him, "Mr. V." Mr. V was hired, fired, and rehired by MacArthur several times while I was there. I understood that when the carousel broke down in the cocktail lounge — which it did quite often — Mr. V was the only person who knew how to put it back together again. With all the maintenance people we had working around the hotel, one would have thought that someone might be able to do the job. But, no, only Mr. V had the smarts to do it.

Once Mr. V tore down the thing to repair it, I could understand why it had to be someone with a special talent to repair it. Endless gears were inside, and it, also, must've had some kind of timing mechanism, since it rotated precisely once every hour.

Anyway, weeks would go by, and I wouldn't see hide nor

hair of Mr. V. Then, I would ask others working around the hotel, "What happened to Mr. V? "

The answer was invariably, "Oh, he'll show up one of these days."

Sure enough, when the carousel stopped working, Mr. V would show up, and MacArthur would evidently hire him all over again to fix the carousel.

Likewise, in our cast of characters was Jimmy the Barber, an elderly gentleman. In fact, he was such a gentleman, he insisted on cutting my hair for nothing. I'd try to tip him. But he'd never take money from me. Then, I'd say, "Jimmy, come on, this is ridiculous! You have to make a living — just like everyone else."

His response: "Yeah, I do. But I do pretty good here. Actually I'm a convenience for the guests, and Mr. MacArthur has let me stay in this shop — never charged me rent or anything. So, I do okay."

As one sat in the barber chair, one couldn't help noticing the walls in the shop. The walls were plastered with postcards and letters from all over the world. Jimmy told me that at one time he'd had 26 chairs going in a big barbershop in New York's Grand Central Station, and he had many tales to tell. I always enjoyed having Jimmy cut my hair.

Next came Sam the Gardener. Sam was a nice man. I'd see him on the grounds in the morning, lugging those big hoses around on that spacious lawn behind the Colonnades. It was his job to take care of the lawn, the waterfalls, all of the property; and it was a big job.

Sam was the same age as Mr. MacArthur. Though a little guy, he was strong as an ox and never complained about anything. Along toward the second year of my employment, MacArthur moved Sammy over to the Yacht Club that MacArthur owned not far from the hotel.

At that time, I was living at the Yacht Club. It was a good deal for me. Mr. MacArthur gave me a studio apartment on the third floor. I paid $50 a week, and Mr. MacArthur paid the utilities.

The Yacht Club had a Chinese restaurant on the second floor. Meanwhile, on the ground floor, there was a full service restaurant and lounge. As a result, I had no reason to leave the island. But back to Sammy.

Sammy was going nuts at the new job. Why? The property needed little or no maintenance. There were no spacious lawns to take care of — almost nothing. Oh, he worked around the pool a little, swept the sidewalks, but that was it.

Usually, I ran home about 12:30 for lunch each day, and I'd encounter Sammy sweeping the sidewalks. Sammy would always say, "Bob, why do you think Mr. MacArthur put me over here? I don't like it over here. There's nothing to do. I loved it over at the hotel."

My response would be, "Yes, I know you loved the hotel, Sammy. I know that. But Mr. Mac is just looking out for you."

I don't think Sammy ever bought that story. In truth, Mr. MacArthur understood that Sammy was growing older and needed a rest. He was, in essence, trying to help and protect a loyal employee — which he did, until the day Sammy died.

Another character was a Cuban by the name of Felipe A. Catasus — nicknamed Phil. Phil had been in command of the Cuban Air Force, prior to Fidel Castro taking over Cuba, and he was MacArthur's personal pilot. Whenever Mr. Mac wanted to fly to his ranch — located about 50 miles northwest of Palm Beach Gardens and bordering on Lake Okeechobee — Phil would fly him there. Meantime, talking to Phil was almost impossible. He spoke broken English that didn't ring much of a bell with me. But we did share a personal joke.

A convention was set up right after I began working at the hotel — a Baptist convention. Mr. Mac called me to his table and said, "You know, we have a big religious convention coming in. It's going to be between 600-to-700 people.

"How long are they going to be here?" I asked.

"For the weekend," he said, as if he had a bad taste in his mouth.

"Well, that's not too bad — "

"Not too bad? What do you mean by that? It's terrible. It's already booked, and there's nothing I can do about it, though."

I still didn't get the gist of the conversation. If he couldn't do anything about it, then who could?

He looked at me intently and said, "I don't know where all those people stole enough money to stay in my hotel. But they obviously stole it from somebody, somewhere."

I smiled inwardly; even at this late date, long after his father's passing, he couldn't resist taking a potshot at religion. But, of course, I said nothing, except "Are you going to be here, Mr. MacArthur?"

"Hell, no!" he said. "I'm taking Phil, and I'm flying to the ranch. I'll be gone the whole weekend. Good luck to you, Bob!"

From then on, every time I saw Phil he would remind me of that story, saying, "Hey, Bob, how about that convention?" Then, he would laugh like crazy and walk away.

Another character was our security guard, Skip. Skip was a tall good-looking guy, well-built, about six feet four inches tall. The problem with Skip was that he never looked like a security guard; fact is, he might have been the general manager walking around the premises. Skip always wore nice suits, and he didn't talk much.

However, Skip hung around the bar at night in case of trouble, though we seldom had trouble at the bar. Nonethe-

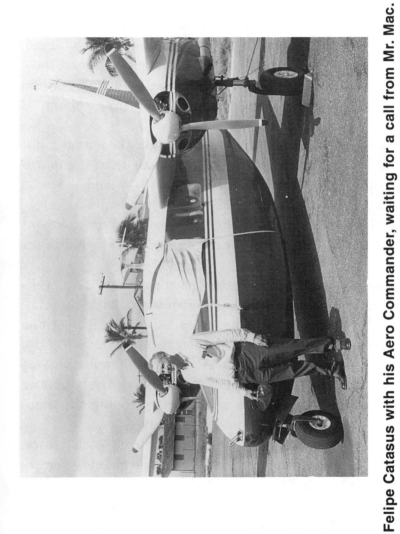

Felipe Catasus with his Aero Commander, waiting for a call from Mr. Mac.

Permission: Felipe A. Catasus

less, as in any bar, from time to time, folks would get a bit loud, and Skip was always smooth as silk in handling the situation. He'd go over and whisper in the offending individual's ear and within a few minutes that person would leave. With Skip, it was just that quick and simple. Since he had so little to do, in time, he loosened up and talked with me.

One night after a minor episode along the lines I have described, I called him over to the bar and said, "Skip, when you whisper in a person's ear, what do you say to them?" I was really impressed by his efficiency.

"I tell them that they don't have to leave the lounge right now, but if they don't, they're going to wake up in the morning with the worst headache of their life . . . And it works every time." Just the thought of it made him smile.

I couldn't disagree with him; throughout my employment at the Colonnade that whisper in the ear never failed to accomplish what Skip expected.

Later, it was an early Sunday morning, I saw Skip, well-dressed as usual, out on the back lawn with a rifle in hand. He was shooting away at some trees. Alarmed, I imagined complaining guests pouring out of their rooms to throttle Skip. Meanwhile, I couldn't imagine what Skip thought he was doing. Finally, after about 25 minutes, Skip gave it up and entered the bar. I said, "Skip, what are you doing out there shooting up the place on a Sunday morning?"

"Oh, Mr. MacArthur is having problems with crows. They're bothering his ducks. He told me to get rid of the crows the best way I could."

I laughed and said, "Well, that sounds about right to me." Heaven forbid that anything should disturb the ducks!

Another episode involving Skip concerned the hotel's newest addition, a building, at the far north side of the property. As I recall, it was December 1976, and the plan was to get the place furnished and ready to open by January first to take advantage of the winter season.

It was a very nice building, complete with a health spa on the ground floor, swimming pool on the ocean side, cabanas, etc. Mr. MacArthur had just had television installed in each and every room throughout the complex. A big football game was coming up in Miami.

Well, sir, he decided to rent out the building, rent out all rooms, for a flat rate for one evening to guests who wanted to see the game. It seemed like a good idea, but it ran into serious problems. People came from all over, and Skip was the only security guard on duty that night.

In the bar, I also had the game on television; and we stayed busy throughout the evening. Somewhere around midnight Skip came into the lounge with a long face. "How's your night going, Bob?"

"Great! Couldn't be better!"

He grimaced and groaned. "I wish I could say the same."

"What's the matter?"

"Well, Miami lost the game — and our guests trashed the new building. When the game was over, they all left as fast as they could." Here he took a deep breath, as if running out of steam. "You wouldn't have believed it. Every room was packed with people, and, of course, they were drinking. There wasn't a damn thing I could do — all by myself — to make a difference."

"Geez," I muttered.

"When you close the bar just take a walk next door, and I'll show you what I'm talking about."

Well, when I finally saw it all I couldn't believe it. It was worse than Skip had said. People had set fires in some of the rooms, punched holes in the walls, even thrown televisions sets through windows into the swimming pool below. "Mr.

MacArthur is going to be bullshit when he hears about this — "

"Well," said Skip, "I'm not going to call him tonight. All the fires are out, everybody's gone, there's nothing I can do right now. I'm going home. I had quite a night."

I couldn't wait to get into the hotel the next day to see what MacArthur's reaction would be to the wholesale destruction. I deliberately walked by his table and said, in passing, "Too bad about what happened last night."

Much to my surprise, he said, "Hell, that was great! Do you know how much publicity I'll get from this? There'll be television cameras all over this place. Anyway, it's covered by insurance."

Still, I couldn't believe his reaction, since if the destruction was covered by insurance, it was probably his insurance company. But he loved the idea of all that publicity. Maybe paying off on the claim was worth it!

Molly Campany, an important member of the cast of characters, ran the coffee shop in the hotel. Well, that was her main job. She did more than that, though — a little of everything. Truth is, she was somewhat like Mr. Mac's Girl Friday. She was especially helpful also during the busy season when we had banquets, functions and parties going on everywhere. Without her, I don't know what I would have done.

Molly was a hard-working Scottish lady. She spoke with a beautiful accent — almost lyrical. I loved listening to her. I remember most of all a story she told me about Mr. MacArthur and his Christmas presents.

During the Christmas season, Mr. MacArthur would get presents from all over the world.

I said to Molly, "What kind of presents?"

"I don't know —"

"You don't know?"

"He doesn't open them."

**Molly Campany, a longtime employee
of the Colonnades Beach Hotel,
holding a bottle of MacArthur Scotch.**

Property of Bob Sanford (February 1995).

That stumped me. "But — but what does he do with them?"

"He throws them in the closets upstairs in his apartment."

"And he doesn't ever open them?" I was disbelieving, I guess.

"No. He can't be bothered with that."

"That's still mighty strange — "

"Yes. But what would you buy for one of the richest men in the world?"

Molly had me there; I was stumped.

All of which reminds me of the Christmas bonus. Sorry, if I digress. But this is worth remembering. All the department heads at the hotel qualified for a Christmas bonus from John D. MacArthur. Each Christmas we would each receive a $12.00 gift certificate from a local Publix supermarket — which basically boiled down to a free turkey for the holidays. I often laugh about that when I think of all of those no doubt lavish gifts that languished in his closets.

Perhaps the funniest story Molly ever told me had to do with Mr. Mac's Weimaraner dog, Zek. When I arrived at the hotel, all kinds of tales were going the rounds about Zek and how Mr. MacArthur had acquired the dog. Everyone agreed Zek, though sleek, tan and handsome as all get out, was a robust nuisance, weighing in at about 60 pounds — to the guests, the employees, you name it. That dog was a constant conversational piece — how Zek came behind the bar and pestered the bartender, ran around the kitchen, chased the ducks all over the beautiful lawn. Molly told me Zek had been a gag gift from New York businessman, Bill Zeckendorf, and that explained how the dog got its name.

"During those days," she said, "it wasn't uncommon for Mr. MacArthur and Mr. Zeckendorf to be doing things like that — back and forth — trying to get one another's goat."

One morning the coffee shop was full of guests. A gentleman was at a table, reading his newspaper over breakfast, Zek came up to his table, snatched a slice of bacon from the gentleman's plate and ran off into the corner.

Mr. MacArthur and Molly were sitting at a table nearby. Said Molly, "Did you see what the dog did?"

Mr. Mac replied, "I did. But I don't think the gentleman noticed it."

"But what will we do, if he complains?" Molly asked.

Mr. MacArthur thought about it for a minute. "Well, that's simple. If he complains, just deduct one slice of bacon from his bill!"

Molly took a trip to Buck Island, the ranch that MacArthur owned in the middle of the state. It all began this way. Mr. Mac came to Molly, saying, "How would you like to fly to the ranch with me today?"

Of course, Molly loved the idea. She had always been curious about the ranch.

As they were flying to the ranch, Mr. Mac said, "Now, Molly, look out through those windows and look at that land as far as you can see."

Molly did as directed.

Then, Mr. Mac said, pointing through the window, "Look in that direction there and look at that land as far as you can see it.

Molly did.

"I own it all," said Mr. Mac..

"Really?" Molly was wide-eyed.

"Yep. Bought it all for a dollar an acre."

Molly marveled, "A dollar an acre." Nothing, she guessed, could top that.

When they landed at the ranch and began to look around,

Molly was awed by the cowboys. "They're real, aren't they?"

"For chrissakes, woman, what do you expect to find on a ranch?" Mr. Mac demanded.

"But I've never seen real cowboys before, Mr. Mac," Molly said. "Except in the movies."

Molly had been employed at the hotel when Mr. Mac purchased it. Molly had never seen MacArthur before, had no idea who he was, how much money he had or anything else. But Molly carried on, as if nothing had changed. Then, MacArthur came into the coffee shop, casually dressed at best, and sat down.

Molly poured him a cup of coffee, and he gave her a little pinch, whereupon Molly promptly went to a hotel employee standing in the corner and said, "Did you see what that man did to me?"

The employee replied, "Do you know who that man is?" Molly didn't.

"That's John D. MacArthur. He owns this place."

Said Molly, "I don't give a rat's ass who he is. He has no right to do that to me." With that, she hurried off to face up to MacArthur at his table. "Excuse me. I don't think you had a right to do that to me. I don't know you."

Mr. Mac looked at her, saying, "You wouldn't happen to be Scottish, would you?"

"I certainly am. I was born and raised in Scotland."

Instantly they formed a common bond, and they remained friends until MacArthur's death.

Molly worked long and hard, that's for sure. I was working up to 15 hours a day, but Molly worked longer. She arrived at the coffee shop at 5:30 in the morning. Some nights, during season with all the functions going on, I would still see her there at ten o'clock at night. If she ever took a day off for herself, I never saw it.

Molly was the one person who had access to Mrs. MacArthur's apartment. In fact, she was one of the few people allowed there. Mrs. MacArthur had her own apartment, while Mr. MacArthur had his. It was an interesting set up, I thought, perhaps saying something about their marriage. But who knows?

But back to Mary, the only employee I figured worth keeping when I took over the bar.

As it turned out, my judgment was sound. Mary worked for me throughout the time I was at the Colonnades, and when I left the hotel in 1978 she went down the street with me to another hotel and worked with me there.

One day Mary came up to me with a paperback book in hand. "Bob," she said, "you find Mr. Mac quite interesting, don't you?"

I couldn't deny it.

"How would you like to have a copy of this book?" She handed it to me.

The title was *The Stockholder.* I studied the cover and said, "This is an unauthorized publication. But, yeah, I wouldn't mind having a copy. I'd at least like to read it.

"It's for you," she said. "You keep it. I have two more of them." Here she paused and looked at me. "This is what I want you to do. You put it in a safe place and don't ever lend it out to anybody. There are rumors flying around this hotel right now that Mr. Mac is so upset about that book that he's going to buy up all the copyrights, and it will never be reprinted again."

I took the information with a grain of salt but thanked Mary nonetheless. I did, though, place the book in a safe place, then took it home with me.

A couple of days later, I was passing Mr. Mac's table. I stopped and asked cautiously, "What did you think about that book?"

"What book?"

"The Stockholder."

"Oh, I hate that book. Nothing but a pack of goddamn lies, that's all it was."

I nodded and hurried on. Obviously, it wasn't a subject to be discussed. But now I couldn't wait to read the book.

Once I read the book I guessed what the problem was — it was unauthorized, and he wasn't making any money from it!

Which brings us to the biggest character of all in my cast — John D. MacArthur himself.

A few days after I started work at the hotel, I was doing my bar inventory for the upcoming shift. I noticed we were out of half-and-half, so I went back to the kitchen where we drew our supplies for the bar and asked for a supply of half-and-half. The kitchen was also out of half-and-half, and the chef said there wouldn't be anymore until the next morning.

In a hotel the size of the Colonnades, it wasn't unusual to get calls for drinks that used half-and-half — Brandy Alexanders, Grasshoppers, etc. I decided I better get some half-and-half before I needed it.

Since I had not been given permission to purchase anything from a store, and I certainly didn't want to bother MacArthur with such a petty matter, I was reluctant to address the subject to him. On the other hand, I felt that we must have half-and-half. Finally, I went over to Mr. MacArthur and explained my dilemma.

"Did you check in the kitchen?"

"They're out — until tomorrow morning.

"Okay. Don't worry about it, Bob. I'll take care of it."

I returned to the bar to wait on customers. Actually, as time wore on, I forgot about the half-and-half, since I'd had no need for it. Then, Mr. MacArthur came into the bar, carrying a little brown bag. He called me to the end of the bar and said, "Now, Bob, this is not exactly what you wanted. But if you mix this stuff with the milk machine in the kitchen, I don't think anybody will know the difference."

I thanked him profusely, and off he went.

Meanwhile, I was shocked that he'd taken his own time, gone to the store and picked it up himself. I opened the bag. Inside were two cans of Pet evaporated milk!

Well, there was no way I was going to use that in drinks. So, I placed them in the very back of the cabinet underneath the bar and beckoned for the bellman. I gave him some money from my own pocket and told him, "At your convenience, go over to the grocery and get me one quart of half-and-half to get us through the night — and mum's the word."

Mr. MacArthur never knew what I did. Those two cans of Pet evaporated milk were probably there when the hotel was torn down years later.

In my cast of characters, I specially like to remember the two ladies from Palm Beach Shores, who came into the lounge almost every afternoon for cocktails. They always sat in the same two seats; and I always served them the same two drinks. It had become a ritual.

Anyway, Mr. MacArthur appeared in the lounge one afternoon, while they were there. I saw him embrace them like old friends. Then, one of the ladies motioned to me and said, "Bob, please give Mr. MacArthur a drink and put it on our check."

I made his usual MacArthur Scotch on the rocks and handed it to him. He accepted gratefully, raised his glass in the air in a toast to these wonderful women, who had been patronizing the lounge since it opened.

After making some small talk with the ladies, Mr. MacArthur glanced at his watch and said, "Well, I guess it's time for me to retire for the evening. It's been a long day." He set his empty glass on the bar and headed for the lobby.

The lady, who'd bought him the drink, called after him, "We bought you a drink!"

Mr. MacArthur paused and turned back to them. "Indeed, you did, and I thank you very much for that."

Taken aback, the lady demanded, "Well, aren't you going to reciprocate?"

Mr. MacArthur replied gravely, "Ladies, you must understand. I sell liquor. I don't buy it."

So much for the cast of characters!

Chapter 6

Playing the Game and Getting Acquainted

Mr. MacArthur had told Mr. K to leave me alone, assuring him that I knew my job. At first, I had thought Mr. K was the general manager. But the hotel had a lot of general managers that came and went, while Mr. K stayed on. Meanwhile, it was easy for me to see that Mr. K was very close to Mr. MacArthur, and he was indeed a crackerjack at sales.

I don't think Mr. K disliked me. But I do believe he was a bit ticked off at the fact that MacArthur had hired me without consulting him. Also, I sensed in a serious way that Mr. K didn't approve of me having the only key to the liquor room and being the lone person responsible for what went in and came out of that room. Here's why.

Every time Mr. K wanted something from the liquor room, he had to go through me. But he always stood by while I made note of anything leaving the room. He must've thought to himself: My only hope is that Bob won't work out.

Once in awhile, Mr. K came to the bar and inquired, "How long do you think you're going to be around here, Bob?"

My answer was always the same: "I figure I'll be around here as long as Mr. MacArthur wants me to be."

In time, though, Mr. K became more friendly. I think he

realized that even though he had no control over me, he also didn't have to worry about the beverage department any longer. He understood that I had all bases covered, and that was what was important to him. In other words, I made him look good. Yet, I'm confident he wanted me under his wing and not MacArthur's. A couple of incidents pointed this out to me vividly.

We had a big party coming up at the hotel, not unusual. Mr. K came to the bar and mentioned the party, asking, "Are you ready for it?"

"Certainly."

"Well, I think maybe on this one, Bob, you might want to bring an extra girl in — just to make sure we're covered."

"No problem," I said; and I immediately got right on it.

I hurried off to my office where I kept a list of people available to work functions. On my first call, I struck pay dirt, and the deed was done, all arrangements made.

Sometime that afternoon, Mr. K came to the bar again. He had in tow a pretty girl. I didn't think much about it, since all the girls found Mr. K irresistible. "Bob," he said, "I want you to meet this girl. She's going to be helping you out with this party we discussed earlier."

I was taken aback. "But you told me to take care of finding someone, and I've already found someone."

The girl dropped her head, embarrassed.

Mr. K. said, "All you have to do is call that girl back and tell her we already have someone. Just apologize, and that'll be that."

I was feeling stubborn now. "I'm not going to do that. You told me to get it covered, and I got it covered."

Mr. K. turned, the girl tagging behind him, and off he went, no doubt madder than a wet hen. But I wasn't about to let him massage his authority over me.

The following morning I went to Mr. K and said, "Don't ever do that to me again. That was very embarrassing, not only for me, but for that poor girl."

"Sorry," he said somewhat reluctantly. "I didn't realize you took care of things that quickly."

Apparently, Mr. K was in charge of hiring the entertainment; and I was glad of that. It gave me one less thing to worry about. Meantime, we had an excellent piano player on the carousel. On this particular day in question, she was due to come in at five o'clock. Then, Mr. K came to me and said, "Bob, do you see this telephone number here? I want you to call the piano player and tell her that we will not be needing her services anymore."

"Excuse me?" I said.

"Oh, come on, Bob. Just give her a call and tell her not to bother to come in. We'll send her the check for whatever we owe her."

"I can't do that — "

"Sure you can. What's the big deal?"

He had me cornered, and I didn't know what else to do. So, yeah, I called the woman, put it to her as nicely as possible and felt bad about it, so bad, the minute I was off the phone, I went to Mr. K and said, "Look. I did what you asked this time. But this is the first and last time. When you hire the entertainment, if you don't like them, you get rid of them."

After that, Mr. K became much more friendly. From then on, when Mr. K came around I just mentioned it to Mr. MacArthur.

Mr. Mac would sometimes say, "Bob, don't listen to him. You have any problems, you just come to me;" or "You know, Bob, the best thing Mr. K says is with his mouth closed."

Just thinking about the lady piano player, though, reminds me of a funny story.

When I arrived one morning, the carousel was all torn up. Mr. V and the whole maintenance department were hovering over it, and it was only eight o'clock. Sometime around 2:00 in the afternoon, I approached Mr. Mac at his table and said, "How long is this going to go on?" nodding toward the carousel.

"Don't know. Could be days." He didn't seem a bit disturbed by the prospects.

"Maybe I should tell Mr. K to call the piano player and tell her what's going on and to reschedule her."

"We'll do no such thing," Mr. Mac said sternly. "We'll just have them take the piano off the carousel, put it in front of the bar, and she can play right there."

Sure enough, about 3:45 p.m., the piano player arrived in the lounge, came up to the bar and said, "I guess you won't be needing me tonight."

I told her that I'd discussed it with Mr. Mac and that the "show must go on". Meanwhile, the piano had been moved, and the piano player went to work.

A few minutes later, Mr. Mac walked in and sat at a table across from the bar. He ordered his usual scotch; a big grin graced his face, and his foot was tapping to the music. He thought everything was going great guns evidently — and it was wonderful.

The carousel was in shambles still, the drills and saws were going, and the piano player was giving it her best shot. Mr. Mac liked action. And this was action in its finest form.

As time went by, I learned much about Mr. K which helped me to understand him better. He had started out as a lifeguard at the hotel while still in school. Then, he left the hotel — I don't know under what terms — and went to work in the Bahamas with one of his brothers who was in charge of a big hotel chain down there. A big fire ensued, and they had to evacuate all of the guests. Within 24-hours, Mr. K had all of those people transported to the Colonnades Beach Hotel — which was almost empty at the time.

Mr. MacArthur, of course, was delighted by this turn of events, and he was also proud of Mr. K and his accomplishments. So, back came Mr. K to the Colonnades, and he was sort of like the Rock of Gibraltar around there — unmovable.

Mr. Mac told me once, "I don't want to give Mr. K the satisfaction of telling him that he's the general manager, even though I think he is every bit as good as any we've ever had."

Meanwhile, general managers came and went with astounding speed. Usually, it was Molly who would tell me when a new general manager was expected. Since I knew that a general manager has to start at the kitchen and the bar, I always made it a point to come in on those days at 7:00 in the morning to get the bar shipshape before a new general manager arrived. As a result, I came up smelling like a rose.

Whatever, as a department head, I had to attend staff meetings. A new general manager arrived, and a staff meeting was called. After a while, it became a huge joke with all of us. The poor guy would get up and say, "My name is so and so, and this is what we're going to do. I hope it's going to be great for the hotel and great for you and great for me." It was like a litany.

Often I wondered why Mr. MacArthur needed a general manager at all; and, yes, why when we got a new one the guy never lasted long. Mr. Mac always gave them a free room and three meals a day. However, I don't know how much he paid them — probably not much. Sometimes I thought he used them just to pick their brains. Regardless, we had a constant ebb and flow of general managers, none of whom seemed to last long enough to accomplish much of anything.

I heard that Mr. Mac was a great chess player. I sometimes thought he played people in the same way. It was a little game he had going, and perhaps the general managers were the chess pieces.

Occasionally I felt I might be part of one of his chess games. A crazy thing happened. Mr. K called me into his office and said, "Bob, you know this new general manager we got. He's going to make it hard for you, and he's going to make it hard for me. Now what we got to do here is — we got to stick together."

"Oh?"

"Yeah, we do. God has been real good to me. I've made a lot of money. I have got a lot of good things going for me. I really wouldn't want to lose this job, though. So, I might need your help."

Carefully I asked, "What can I do for you?"

He was ready for me. "I'm going to bring the new general manager into the bar tonight. What I would like you to do is every time he orders a drink — load it up good. Then, make mine half of what I usually have."

I nodded. "Okay. I'll do that," thinking all the while that here was another chess game.

Back at the bar, as I worked, I couldn't get this business of loading up the new general manager with booze off my mind. After some thought, I figured that probably many of these general managers would like to deep-six Mr. K. After all, he carried a bunch of clout with Mr. Mac.

The next day I heard Mr. K talking with Mr. Mac. He was saying, "I understand your general manager was in pretty bad shape when he left the hotel last night."

Within 24 hours the general manager was gone.

So, there were all kinds of little games being played. If you wanted to stay on at the hotel, you needed to learn how to play the game. As I saw it, the game was really pretty simple. Mr. Mac remembered everything you told him that you planned to do, and it was best not to lose track of that fact.

For instance, if you said, "Mr. MacArthur, I'll be here at eight o'clock every morning," you damn well better be there. If you began missing your own deadline, you were as good as gone and rather soon too.

In the beginning, the hotel wasn't too busy. But as the busy winter season approached, it was time to speak with Mr. Mac about putting on an extra bartender. I knew just who I wanted to hire, and I hired him. Then, I sat down at Mr. Mac's table in the coffee shop and said, "I hired a bartender in Tampa. He was with me over there for three years. His name is Mickey Wheeler. He's a real hard worker, and I think he'll be great for us. Here's the deal. If you let me send for him, between the two of us, we'll cover all the bar shifts. It will probably mean seven days a week for us both, but we'll do it."

"Just the two of you? Nobody else?" He seemed surprised.

"That's right."

"Bob, bring him on board — and don't let me down."

I promised I'd not let him down.

After Mickey came in from Tampa and got his feet on the floor, every once in a while Mr. Mac would call me to his table and say, "Looks like you two have got things covered;" and that's what mattered to him — I had kept my word.

Mr. K, along with some of his friends in Canada, had set up a program with Treasure Tours to bring in Canadian tourists to the hotel for a week or more. The program was very successful. As I saw it, we were getting almost 250 Canadian guests per week.

On Sundays Mickey and I had to make up a 20-gallon bucket of punch for the arriving guests and their orientation party in The Bob Hope Suite . We called it, "Change over day," since guests were leaving and a whole new batch was arriving. Mr. K was in charge of all of this, and he was a master at it.

Actually, what it boiled down to was this. Mr. K would welcome the guests to the property and tell them what was available to them during their stay. This program was set up, so that one person — for $239.00 — received a plane ticket from Canada to Florida and back, lodging and meals at the hotel, and the privilege of using the PGA golf courses Mr. MacArthur owned.

The regular guests didn't care too much for this at first — sharing their hotel with a lot of tour people. But eventually it became an interesting blend of people. Meanwhile, one couldn't help noticing that about 80 percent of the Canadians were young, attractive women, all of which made it easier to bear, I'm sure. In fact, the carousel bar became the talk of the town. Guys congregated there to look over, date, ask out the good-looking Canadian gals.

One day Mickey and I were out at the tiki bar on the ocean; women were everywhere.

Mickey looked at me and said, "Bob, there's no way we can stay married working at this hotel."

I laughed and said, "You're probably right, Mickey." Distractions were everywhere on that beach.

Mickey and I worked out just as I had said we would. Unfortunately, unbeknownst to me, Mickey was not in good health, and it started to show. He began missing shifts, and I was working around the clock to cover both shifts. After a few weeks, though, Mickey came to me and said he was sorry; he should return to Tampa to be with his family. He never discussed the nature of his illness with me. But within a month of his return to Tampa, his mother called me, saying,

"Mickey's gone." She then thanked me for being a good friend. I did miss him.

A week later, I brought in a new bartender, Jack Penrose, who was well known in the area. Jack was acquainted with Mr. MacArthur and Mr. K. I felt sure I wouldn't have to tell him how to play the game.

Shortly thereafter, I was going through the big liquor room. I had about a $3500.00 inventory there. As I stopped to look back through the order sheets, underneath I found a brown envelope. I opened the envelope and inside were fifteen brand-new keys, giving real pause for thought. I wondered if one of those keys — or all of them — would fit the liquor room door.

At the Colonnades the liquor room was located outside the main building. So, it would have been possible for someone, if they knew where the security guard was, to back a vehicle up next to the liquor room, open their trunk, open the liquor room door and help themselves to the booze. I tried everyone of those keys in that door lock — and bingo! — they all fit.

Immediately I brought the envelope with the keys inside to Mr. Mac's attention.

His response was one of surprise, though he took it calmly. "I guess that's what's going on around here. Thank you, Bob, and keep up the good work."

Well, one thing for sure, nobody could complain about me shirking my duty. I spent so much time at the hotel, working, even my wife was beginning to complain. Yet, she had a point. All that beautiful ocean was out there, and we never enjoyed it. But I had made a deal with Mr. Mac, and as far as I was concerned: A deal is a deal.

Perhaps I just wanted to meet Mr. Mac's challenge; I don't know. But I was proud of myself, and I wanted Mr. Mac to be proud of me. I had never had a cross word with or from the man, and I appreciated this kind of consideration.

For instance, he might have spent the day talking with a long line of people who'd been waiting to see him. Once they were out of the way, he might say to me, "Bob, come and sit down." Then, he'd start asking me questions, and sometimes we'd just talk for perhaps up to half an hour about nothing really important. He was a very interesting man, I learned. I enjoyed listening to him, and he always seemed just as pleasant and interested in what I had to say.

Over the years, I met some truly interesting people at the hotel. Paul Harvey, the radio commentator, was one of them This man simply towered over me. He must have been at least six feet four inches tall. When he shook my hand I was relieved when he let my hand go. What a grip!

Along with Harvey, I did meet Jack Nicklaus, Helen Hayes — Mr. Mac's very famous actress sister-in-law — Johnny Weismuller, the original Tarzan, and many others when they visited the Colonnades — all interesting personalities. Perhaps one stands out more than others, though. He came into the bar during the afternoon and ordered a drink. I couldn't help noticing a large ring on his finger. Curiosity got the best of me, and I said, "Excuse me, sir. That's quite a ring you have there."

He took it off and handed it to me. "Have you ever seen a ring like this before?"

I hadn't. I examined the ring more closely. By golly, it was a World Series ring. I handed the ring back to him and introduced myself, eyes wide and admiring, saying, "Wow!"

"I'm Dick Williams," he said. Then, he proceeded to tell me about how he had managed the Boston Red Sox. In fact, he told me a story about how Mr. Mac had given him a job at the hotel as a public relations man during off seasons. "Why," said Mr. Williams, "he even gave me a little office. I really loved that job. Didn't have to do anything but talk to the guests, shake hands and sign autographs."

Mr. MacArthur might have had a soft spot in his heart for the so-called important people of this world, but perhaps he rose to new heights when it came to the handicapped. At one time we had a piano player who was a paraplegic — his name was Tony. Tony thought the world of Mr. Mac, and I sensed that Mr. Mac thought the world of Tony. Mr. Mac would always come out and greet Tony. Then, he'd sit down on the carousel and listen to Tony play.

Tony was an amazing man. He drove all the way up from Fort Lauderdale every afternoon, started playing at six o'clock, departed at two o'clock in the morning, and drove all the way back to Lauderdale. You just had to admire the guy!

Another fellow who worked at the hotel that I admired was Cooper, a black man. Coop had a personality that wouldn't quit; and it was bigger than he was. Though not overly tall, Coop was built like a ton of bricks. He was always laughing and joking, genuinely an upbeat fellow. Everyone liked him; he was an inspiration to one and all. Meanwhile, he was never late — always early. And Mr. Mac recognized not only his punctuality but his dedication to the hotel.

Perhaps the most interesting convention we had was the Barber Shop Quartet Convention. These people came from all around the country that summer. Too bad it was the off season — because having these folks around made for a ball. They sang all day; and they sang all night during their weekend stay. It didn't matter what section of the hotel you were in. People were singing. As I recall, there were approximately 600 in attendance. It was a beautiful thing to behold, and I'll never forget it.

On several occasions, I met Mr. MacArthur's top people

from Chicago. Now and then, he'd invite them all down to Florida to spend the weekend. I remember meeting Bill Kirby, who later assisted Mr. Mac in setting up the John D. and Catherine T. MacArthur Foundation, Paul Doolen, and Louis Feil, though many other names escape me.

During one of these get-togethers, I was setting up the bar around noon. In the dining room employees were putting tables together. In about half an hour, a dozen or so of these guys from Chicago came into the lobby. They were all dressed in "MacArthur plaid sport coats — the plaid, the Tartan of the MacArthur Clan". It was an honor to wear one of those green and yellow plaid coats with the MacArthur family crest on the breast pocket; in fact, embroidered in gold lettering on the crest was the Latin phrase, *Fide et Opera,* meaning "faith and work" which — in MacArthur's words meant, "Be honest and work like a son of a bitch."

I must say they were quite an impressive sight in those sport coats with white shirts and ties as they sat around the table, the head of the table going unoccupied, until The Skipper, Mr. MacArthur, came in, dressed, as usual, in an open white shirt and an old maroon sweater. He sat at the head of the table, he beckoned to me and drinks were ordered. As I hurried away, he picked up the telephone.

From where I stood in the bar, mixing drinks for Mr. Mac's guests, I saw that he was looking across the lawn to the tiki bar. In no time at all the well-endowed bar maid from the tiki bar was coming toward the hotel, dressed as usual in a very revealing string bikini. She entered the dining room went to Mr. Mac's table, and the next thing I knew — she was sitting in Mr. MacArthur's lap!

I quickly placed all the drinks I'd mixed on a tray and headed for the dining room. I didn't want to miss the show — not even a little bit. By the time I arrived at the table, Mr.

MacArthur was cradling her scantily covered breasts in his hands and was saying, "Now, gentlemen, ain't that a pair of beauties?"

I almost dropped the tray. I shouldn't have. It wasn't uncommon for me to have a bar full of people and for Mr. Mac to walk up behind a lady there and place his hands gently over her breasts. His line was "Don't get nervous. I'm simply checking for cancer."

Even people who knew Mr. Mac well were shocked by this behavior. They'd ask me, "Does he do that sort of thing often?"

I'd hedge my bets and say, "Oh, once in awhile."

The response was always, "Oh, my god!"

People who didn't know him would say, "Who in hell is that dirty old man? What's he doing? How does he get away with that?"

To be honest, I was always shocked by this oddity in his behavior. But as time wore on, I learned to expect it. How he enjoyed doing the unpredictable; and if I were to hazard a guess, I sometimes suspect that's all it amounted to. Others may prove me wrong, but that's how I saw it.

Chapter 7

Mr. Mac and the Queen of England

By now, I was well aware that Mr. Mac didn't care for big, fancy gatherings and other assorted get-togethers, designed to entertain the very rich and very famous. In fact, he avoided them like the plague. For instance, the plaid sport coats his top salesmen and people from Chicago wore — well, that was his idea of dressing up. He'd don a white shirt, tie and one of those plaid sport coats, and he was ready for the best of 'em. Incidentally, those sport coats were made by a mill he owned. Perhaps that's why they were designated attire for his top insurance people. They came cheap or free to him.

If he was forced to "get dressed up" and had to put on his plaid sport coat and travel to, say, Chicago on business, he was down right grumpy about it. I understood on such occasions he always traveled tourist, "since the back of the plane got there at the same time as the front of the plane".

Whatever, as you can see, he simply wasn't up to meeting the Queen of England under any circumstances. But that was about to happen in July 1976, and he was trapped.

The Queen of England was traveling to Washington, D. C. She had, in advance — along with the assistance of President Gerald Ford's staff — made up an highly selective list of distinguished guests to be invited to meet and greet her at a White House dinner. Lo and behold, John D. MacArthur's name was on that list, and he was notified by the powers-that-be with a beautifully engraved invitation that read:

> The President and Mrs. Ford request the pleasure of the company of Mr. John D. MacArthur for dinner on Wednesday evening, July 7, 1976, at 8 o'clock on the occasion of the visit of Her Majesty Queen Elizabeth the Second and His Royal Highness Prince Philip, Duke of Edinburgh.

Mr. Mac, a longtime personal friend of President Ford, couldn't imagine that Ford had a hand in the invitation. Instead he preferred to put this interruption in his busy schedule down to the fact that his service with the British during World War I was the reason for his inclusion in the guest list. However, the part that really got his goat was the notation on the invitation which indicated that only "white tie" was acceptable attire.

For weeks, this was the top story around the hotel, while Mr. Mac went around muttering things about "that dreadful event", which don't bear repeating.

One day I observed Mr. Mac across from the main bar; he was carrying on something fearsome about the cost of renting formal attire, not to mention having to put it on and go to Washington. Actually, I could see the pain in his face as he spoke. Maybe it was more like terror; I don't know. But he damn well didn't want to do what he was going to have to do.

As the days dwindled down to a precious few, prior to his Washington appearance, preparations, involving Mr. Mac's formal attire, were beginning to take shape. It seemed that

Mr. Mac was now in possession of a tuxedo. However, it evidently didn't fit the bill, since he was in need of a tails, white tie and only God knows what else. Frustration was building under these unfortunate circumstances.

During those days, Peter Swanberg owned The Tux Shop on Northlake Boulevard in Palm Beach Gardens. As the story goes, Mr. K called Peter and explained what would be needed, asking if Peter would come to the MacArthur's apartment and take the necessary measurements to outfit Mr. Mac in formal attire.

Here Peter provides our insight into this unholy situation. Peter entered the MacArthur apartment. Mr. MacArthur awaited Peter's arrival — wearing only his birthday suit!

Peter swallowed and said nothing. He was there to do a job, and he did it. He quickly took the measurements and departed.

As soon as Peter returned to his shop, the phone rang. It was Mr. K, thanking him, on one hand, for the trouble he had gone to, and, on the other hand, trying to explain to Peter that it would be a cold day in hell before he saw any money for his efforts.

Peter had heard stories about Mr. MacArthur — what a tightwad he was. Therefore, he wasn't surprised. However, Mr. K did say, "I'll meet you later, and maybe we can work something out."

The end result, via the courtesy of Mr. K and his connections: Peter got to spend seven days at the Jack Tar Village in the Bahamas' west end. As for Mr. Mac asking for a bill and paying same, nothing of the kind occurred.

As for the rest, Peter had saved the day, and the time did arrive when Mr. Mac, in spite of all of his grumbling and carrying on, did go to meet the Queen of England in Washington, D C, dressed better, perhaps, than at any time in his life.

Upon his return to the hotel, the local *Palm Beach Post* ran a feature article about Mr. Mac's trip to Washington. In large bold print, the headline read:

JOHN D. UNIMPRESSED BY HER MAJESTY.

The article contained a couple of priceless quotes from Mr. Mac: "The Queen was beautiful from the crown up," and "I never saw so many diamonds in one pile."

As for Prince Philip, he said, "I thought he was the butler, until someone told me he was the Prince."

In truth, he didn't like much of anything, including the music: "The musicians were simply awful. I was told the Queen liked that kind of music, but I don't know why I had to suffer because she liked that crap."

When asked what he had for dinner, Mr. Mac responded, "I can't recall. The dinner started with a cocktail party, and if you had an empty glass, it didn't stay that way for long. They were really trying to get rid of that stuff, and I was only too glad to help. So, you must forgive me, if I don't remember anything."

Mr. Mac escorted his sister-in-law, the celebrated actress Helen Hayes, who had also been invited to attend. He let Helen handle the curtsy, the formal greeting of the Queen. He, however, did feel, "A handshake was sufficient."

The occasion did have a few saving graces. He enjoyed seeing some old friends, Bob Hope and his wife, Billy Graham, and the former Texas Governor John Connelly. And though he had visited The White House previously, this was his "first free meal" there!

Despite all the grousing and the costs involved, such as having had to wear his first "monkey suit", Mr. Mac was honored and proud to have attended the dinner. "There were only

200 in the nation invited," he said, grinning. "That makes me one in a million!"

If one were to translate this into something other than MacArthur-speak, he was saying,

"It was a unique experience; and I enjoyed myself immensely."

Since he was a marvelous storyteller, I'm confident that he whiled away many an hour regaling folks he encountered with the events of that memorable evening.

Chapter 8

Confrontations with Mr. Mac

Though Mr. Mac and I never exchanged cross words, on occasion, when I did things he didn't like, he made sure I knew it — pronto.

I was at home, during my noon break from the bar, prior to going back to open the bar later that afternoon. Mr. Mac phoned and said, "Bob, can you get right over here?"

"Sure," I said, "I'll be right there." I couldn't imagine what was up. My drive to the hotel was probably the longest of my life. Mr. Mac had never telephoned me before at home. And, of course, I imagined the worst. Upon arrival, I went directly to Mr. Mac's table.

Said Mr. Mac, "I had some people here from Chicago. I wanted to give them a case of my MacArthur Scotch, and you have the only key to the liquor room." It was almost an accusation of some wrong done.

I apologized profusely, then said, "However, if you'll remember, it was your idea that I have the only key. Perhaps we could make another arrangement. Maybe we could keep the key locked up somewhere around here, so that if you wanted to get into the liquor room at any time, it would be no problem."

He paused for the longest time, slow, but deliberating a decision, as was sometimes his nature. Finally, he said, "No, let's keep things the way they are. It's water over the dam anyway."

Then, he added, "Bob, I'm sorry to have bothered you about that," and he meant it.

After working at the hotel those first few weeks, I had set my mind on making the place look nicer and more attractive to the guests. In the evening, the lounge didn't have much warmth. Except for the carousel, it appeared — cold, cold, cold. Some tables were across from the bar with bench seating, and that area was almost without any kind of intimacy or encouragement. In time, I ordered candles, thinking they might give the bar the warmth it needed.

About a week went by; the candles didn't arrive. I called the company. They assured me that one case of candles had been shipped. I told them, "I didn't receive them." I was about to put in another order when the thought came to me that I should just stand back and see what happened. I suspected a fly in the ointment, since the company had stated in no uncertain terms that the candles had been shipped.

Finally, Mr. K came into the bar. I said. "Do you know anything about a case of candles I ordered?"

"Yeah. And I know what happened to them."

"What happened?" I demanded.

"Mr. MacArthur sent them back."

"Why did he do that?"

"Well, you know Mr. Mac," said Mr. K. "He probably thought it was a waste of money."

That conversation behind me, I hurried off to Mr. Mac's table.

When, I appeared, he looked up at me, waiting.

"Could I please speak with you for a minute?" I asked.

"Sure. Sit down. What's up?"

"It's a small thing," I said. "But I ordered a case of candles. Mr. K said you sent them back."

He nodded. "I did."

"Well, I guess I should have asked your permission before ordering them —"

"What did you want them for?"

"I thought candlelight would make the room a little nicer in the evening — give it some warmth — "

"Oh," he said slowly, "there's no reason for us to have those things. Our air conditioner doesn't work that well anyway. Candles throw off a lot of heat, you know."

I shrugged and said, "You're probably right. Let's just forget it. We don't need them." I started to get up.

"Look, Bob," he said. "Tell you what. If a case of candles turns you on that much, I think you ought to go ahead and order them."

I had candles on those tables, until the time I left the hotel.

Mr. Mac was funny about things like that. I'm sure he thought the candles were a waste of money, in more ways than one. Of course, let's face it, he didn't get as rich as he was by wasting money — that's for sure.

We had a happy hour in the lounge, and that too was definitely a waste of money as far as Mr. MacArthur was concerned. However, when it came to placing little snacks around the bar — popcorn, peanuts, things of that nature — he never seemed to mind.

During the Christmas holiday season, the delivery truck with the snacks arrived early in the morning before I came in. Someone else signed for them. When I checked the invoice I noticed a case of mixed nuts had been sent instead of the dry roasted peanuts I usually received. Geez, I thought;

Mr. Mac'll never stand for this. Mixed nuts were very expensive.

Well, I had to make a decision. I could wait until after the holidays and exchange them, or I could take a chance and use them, hoping Mr. Mac wouldn't notice. I decided to put them out on the bar that evening for a test run.

As luck would have it, that very evening Mr. Mac left his table with his mail under his arm as was his habit, but he came directly to the bar. I held my breath as he moved along the bar and his hand scooped up mixed nuts from a dish there. They must've felt like real jewels in his hand, since he was eating them with relish by the time he came to the end of the bar. Here he paused, though, and motioned for me to come over to him.

I cringed and took the long walk. Boy, I was in trouble up to my arm pits!

Very quietly, Mr. MacArthur asked, "Bob, where did we get these little babies?"

I took a deep breath and responded, "I'll be more than happy to explain all of that to you, Mr. MacArthur. I'll come and talk with you in the morning and tell you exactly what happened."

"You do just that," he said.

Of course, the next morning, I was right there at the table, explaining how those mixed nuts came to be on the bar.

He cocked his head and thought about it, finally saying, "Well, Bob, those nuts are awfully expensive. Just don't let that happen again."

I breathed a sigh of relief; and, naturally it never happened again.

My biggest confrontation with Mr. Mac involved the salesmen from Chicago. They were at the hotel for another weekend, only this time they were to have a party in one of the rooms that we had for functions upstairs in the main building. Of course, all the function sheets were on my desk. These sheets included special orders like liquor we might not normally carry, special bottles of wine, that sort of thing. It was my job to make sure we had these items for such occasions.

On a particular function sheet, I noticed a special order for several bottles of Jack Daniels and several bottles of Crown Royal, and I made sure that this liquor was at the bar for the party. In fact, I worked the party myself that night.

To this point, Mr. Mac had never shown up at any of the evening parties or functions. But wouldn't you know it — he elected to show up for this one. He walked right up to the bar and said, "Bob, why don't you have any of my scotch on the bar?"

"Mr. MacArthur, if I'd known you were going to be here, I'd've had a whole case."

"Forget about that," he said. "What's that Crown Royal and that other brand doing there?"

"It was on the function sheet — "

"I don't give a goddamn about function sheets! Get that stuff out of there right now."

I called downstairs and asked the other bartender to send up an empty box. In a minute or two he arrived, and I placed the offending Crown Royal and Jack Daniels in the box. The bartender took it downstairs.

Once the deed was done, Mr. Mac called me aside and said, "Bob, let's not let that happen again under any circumstances. Function sheet or no function sheet."

"It won't happen again, sir."

Mr. Mac nodded and went on his way, leaving the party behind..

Meanwhile, for the rest of the evening, I heard nothing

but complaints from the salesmen:

"How could The Skipper do a thing like that to us? We're his top salesmen, and we can't even have Crown Royal at our party!" They were just a bit ticked off, as the saying goes.

Most of my confrontations with Mr. Mac were funny. He made them funny. He always complained about the number of cocktail napkins we were using. I think if I could have reported we were using zero napkins that might have made his day. Inevitably, he walked into the bar when he was on a "cocktail napkin tear", took one single napkin from its container, waved it in the air, as if it might be a distress flag, and yelled at me, "Bob, you tell those cocktail waitresses we got a paper shortage going on!"

My response was always "Yes, sir!" as if I might be in the military; and that was the end of that.

Off he would go then — on another mission, no doubt, to beat back waste wherever it might be flourishing; and in his world, well, that was everywhere!

Chapter 9

A Busy Man Indeed

Once upon a time, Mr. MacArthur told me that his biggest fear was to wake up some morning and find he had absolutely nothing to do. From my own observations, I guessed this wasn't likely. He was involved in everything.

Most of his days were consumed with conversations at his table in the coffee shop with people from all over the country. When he was alone at the table, usually he was on the local phone or the WATTS line to his insurance company in Chicago.

I had the pleasure of talking with a man once, who had worked as an insurance salesman for Mr. Mac at Bankers Life and Casualty in Chicago. Said the man, "I don't know what will happen to that company when Mr. MacArthur passes on."

While I knew Mr. Mac took an active role in the management of the company, I never imagined he held the reins that tightly. "What do you mean?"

"No matter what your title is up there or how long you've been there, all the final decisions must come by telephone from Mr. MacArthur himself."

It had never occurred to me that all the final decisions

for that insurance company were made at the little table in the coffee shop of the hotel. After that, I was rather amazed that Mr. Mac had so much time for all those people, not to mention all of us. Nothing escaped his attention.

As if all this might not be enough, now and then, I saw Mr. Mac helping guests into the hotel with their luggage. Sometimes I even saw him helping out in the kitchen when the restaurant was overly busy, as if he might be one of the staff. Sometimes he also assisted the maintenance people outside, putting up or taking down something. He was a truly remarkable man for one in his late 70s.

Yet, in some respects, I thought, Mr. Mac wasn't all that well organized. Those long lines of people in the lobby, waiting for a chance to sit down with him, never had appointments. Nevertheless, he kept the people moving, the pace flowing, in one door and out the other. I could never figure out how he did it, until Molly confided in me that she and Mr. Mac had a system of hand signals. If Mr. Mac had someone at the table that he had no interest in or someone who was boring the socks off of him, he signaled Molly to rescue him. Molly always let a couple of minutes pass. Then, she approached the table and said, "Excuse me, Mr. MacArthur, your next appointment is here now," which gave Mr. Mac a reason for ending the current conversation. One of his favorite saying was:

Time wasted is time lost — gone forever. It's time you will never replace.

The one pause in Mr. Mac's day came at noon. When the hour struck 12:00 he rose from his table, went out the door of the coffee shop and into a room adjacent to that door. At 12:30, he returned to his table.

I said to Molly once, "What does he do in there?"

"He just goes in there to get away from things and rest

his mind. Then, he's ready to get back to business."

And what a marvelous mind it must've been, since he was right on top of everything, and he had his finger in every pie!

But that wasn't the end of it. Molly said, "At five minutes after 12:00, Mrs. MacArthur always calls from her apartment to see if Mr. Mac is resting."

At this time, after three years in the hotel, I still didn't know much about Mrs. MacArthur. In fact, I had only seen her a few times. Once, I recall seeing her at the far end of the property, walking her two poodles. One evening I saw her in the main dining room with Mr. Mac. Another time, and I'll never forget this, since it was Thanksgiving Day, I had been in the kitchen, talking with the chef. When I departed a handsome woman, attired in rather ordinary drip-dry shirt and slacks, was standing by the back door, plate in hand. I didn't think much about it, though she looked familiar to me.

Later I had a reason to return to the kitchen. Suddenly it came to me, and I said to the chef, "Was that Mrs. MacArthur standing by the door, plate in hand?"

"That was her," he said.

"What did she want?" I was truly baffled. I knew that Mr. and Mrs. Mac led an almost Spartan life, going to bed with the chickens, seldom going out, but she had appeared to me, though attractive to the eye, almost as if she might be looking for a hand out.

"Oh, she said she just wanted to know if she could have a little piece of turkey."

Evidently here were two peas in a pod, both thrifty to a flaw!

Sometime later, I was to learn that I was right about her. That was why the two of them were so successful.

Mrs. MacArthur had worked right along beside Mr.

MacArthur in building an empire. She chose to live in her apartment upstairs with its little in-house office where she kept track of everything in the entire hotel. One would have never guessed, since she was almost invisible to the staff.

A case in point:

We were all hustling around getting ready for a New Year's Eve gathering at the hotel.

Molly accosted me with two balloons. She handed them to me, saying, "Mrs. MacArthur brought these down. She said maybe you could use them for your decorations tonight."

I stared at the two limp balloons. "These came from Mrs. MacArthur? She thought they'd be a contribution to the decorations?" Which proved to me that I had been right; Mr. Mac and Mrs. MacArthur *were* two peas in a pod.

All of which reminds me. About a week before that Christmas, Mr. Mac and Molly were in the lobby with a couple of boxes of Christmas decorations. The decorations had been dumped on the floor, and it was a mess, if I do say so. All of a sudden I heard Mr. Mac yelling at the top of his voice, "Don't spend any money!"

I went out to the lobby to see what was going on. I eyed the decorations. They were old as sin. I thought to myself: I'm not getting involved in this fiasco. I turned around and went back to the bar.

Then, I talked about the business of Christmas decorations with a few people who worked with me. We decided to buy our own decorations. Having the only key to the liquor room, I figured we could keep them locked up there between each Christmas, and they would look nice each year. Meanwhile, nobody would know the difference, and we wouldn't have to bother anyone. So, that's exactly what we did, so that we wouldn't have to hear that awful, bloodcurdling yell, "Don't spend any money!"

On that score, one of my favorite stories concerns the carpet in the elevator. The carpet in the elevator was in shreds, worn out, done for. It would have been a small project to replace it. However, Mr. Mac made a very, very small project of it, and the project involved Mr. V, our head maintenance man.

Mr. Mac and Mr. V were standing at the end of the bar, talking. I heard Mr. Mac say to Mr. V, "It's a simple thing to change that carpet in the elevator. Just go up to one of the rooms. Move the bed to one side and cut out a piece of pre-measured carpet. Then, move the bed back in place and put that carpet in the elevator. It's as simple as that. No problem."

An hour or so later, the project was finished — and in the manner Mr. Mac had suggested.

Every once in awhile, when Mr. Mac came to the bar for his drink he took out a shabby, little wallet from his back pocket that was older than Methuselah. Then, he'd pull out a single dollar bill and hand it to me, saying, "Bob, that's for you."

In retrospect, I don't think, in all my life, I've ever received a larger tip. Let's face it.

Talk about tight? Here was the tightest of the tight with more money than God. But he appreciated me enough to tip me —once in a great while, you understand — a whole buck.

Now that was generosity at its best!

I think the most angry I ever saw Mr. Mac, if you could call it anger, was the day he threw the Board of Health representatives from the hotel. They were shouting at Mr. Mac, and Mr. Mac was shouting back — the beginning of World War III in the making, no doubt.

A few weeks after the incident, I was talking to Roger Ross, one of the guys involved; he'd been with the Board of

Health for a number of years. What the Board of Health was trying to do was shut down the hotel for more than one infraction, it seemed. However, they knew who they were up against, and they knew that they could never shut it down — not with Mr. Mac's power and money.

Roger Ross told me, "You know, Bob, they're not going to have to ever tear this hotel down. This place is going to fall down all on its own."

And he was right. Everything was falling apart. Balconies had already fallen off, some of the rooms upstairs had floors that were so warped, walking across them was like a day at sea. Basically, what stayed together was patch, patch, patch work; and often repairs were just a matter of robbing Peter to pay Paul. I crossed my fingers and hoped for the best. A case in point was the day Mr. Mac came into the bar and set a great big box there. "I just cleaned out the bar over at the Biltmore." He had purchased the Biltmore Hotel in Palm Beach, Florida, down the coast, and closed it the same day.

"Oh," I said, wondering what was next.

He started pulling stuff from the box, mainly bar items like shakers and a whole array of different glasses. "Why don't you clean up this stuff," he said, "and put it on the bar? I'm sure you can use it here . . . And, oh, if there's anything in there that you want for yourself personally — just go ahead and take it."

Of course, I thanked him profusely, as if I'd just come into a gold mine.

However, as I cleaned the items up, I did find some very interesting things: four cocktail glasses that were souvenirs from the first PGA Golf Classic in Palm Beach Gardens in 1971. I put these aside for myself. I gave two away to personal friends, one to my father, and I still have the fourth one.

I cherish it; it came to me from Mr. Mac.

As for the remainder of the items, I decided, yes, I could use them in the bar. Hell, I could use almost anything and everything in the bar. True enough, the glasses didn't match what we had, but I figured it would make Mr. Mac happy to see his salvage at work!

Mr. MacArthur and Lee Trevino at PGA National Golf Tournament, Palm Beach Gardens, Florida.

Permission: Bill Wood (early 1970s).

Mr. MacArthur giving a speech at the Colonnades Beach Hotel dinner party for the PGA National Golf Tournament. Hollywood celebrity Bob Hope is seated on Mr. Mac's left.

Permission: Bill Wood (early 1970s).

Chapter 10

The Final Days

As time rolled on, Mr. Mac's health declined. It was no secret that he had emphysema and blood sugar problems. Then, a year prior to his death, he suffered a stroke that paralyzed one side of his body. His speech was also badly impaired. This was so frustrating for him that there's hardly any way to explain it. Meanwhile, all of us who worked for him lost the most important part of the hotel. We had lost the ability to communicate with Mr. Mac.

During that period, I was dating one of Mr. Mac's private nurses. She told me the story of one of his more notorious hospital stays. The gist of it: He felt like he was in a jail where everyone had set out to rip him off financially with all their fancy equipment — oxygen tent, etc., etc., etc. Finally he told the hospital, "I'll buy the stuff," and he did — up to and including a hospital bed to his liking.

At last, the day before he was to be released from this hospitalization, a nurse entered his room to tidy up. Mr. Mac boasted to her, "I'm leaving."

"Oh, no, you're not. You're staying right here."

Furious, Mr. Mac — still in his hospital gown and despite being weak from his ordeal in the hospital — crawled out of bed and headed for the door.

The nurse, much younger and fleet of foot, beat him to the door and bolted it.

Whereupon Mr. Mac picked up a chair and started smashing the window panes, roaring in a defiant voice, "There's more ways than one to get out of here!"

The nurse ran to the door, unlocked it, and screamed for help.

The head nurse came running and kept Mr. Mac from exiting through the now open window — 30 feet down into the parking lot below!

But back to his return from the hospital, after his stroke . . .

He had quit smoking and seldom ordered a scotch. The lectures from his doctors must have been a clarion call.

After his stroke, things were never the same around the hotel. No more long lines of people waited in the lobby. It was as if all the life had been sucked from the Colonnades. Then, a realization came to me. I had had my last real conversation with a man I had come to respect, a man who was far more interesting than 99.9 percent of the people with whom I spoke.

In truth, I became something of a coward when it came to Mr. Mac. When he inched his way toward the bar, every step an effort for him, I avoided eye contact, since having a conversation with him was almost impossible. He spoke with a mumble that was terribly hard to understand; and it broke my heart to see him make the effort — yet, I tried. But still I avoided eye contact. I didn't want him to see how really sorry I was for him.

On January 6, 1978, the final day came. John Donald MacArthur died at Good Samaritan Hospital in West Palm Beach of cancer of the pancreas.

The next day Mr. K had a meeting with all of the staff,

saying, "The Skipper is gone. But it is up to us to keep the ship afloat. It's a new day for the Colonnades Beach Hotel, and I'm going to need all of your help. I'm open to suggestions at any time. Thanks. Let's get back to work."

As I returned to the bar, I remembered something Mr. Mac told me. "Bob," he said, "I have two ambitions in this life. I want to live to be 80 years old, and at that time — I want to be the richest man in the country."

When he died, The Skipper was 80 years old and the second richest man in the United States of America — almost over the hump!

That same day, Mrs. MacArthur said, "The ducks must go," and what a day that turned out to be . . .

I watched the whole thing from the bar through the big windows there. The housekeeping department and the maintenance department chased those ducks, trying to one by one catch them all. What a sight to behold — it was hilarious!

Bob Ratcliffe, a longtime member of the Palm Beach Shores Police Department who had been involved in the hotel's security, told me something about that day to add to the above.

He called his story, *One Lone Duck*.

After housekeeping and maintenance thought all the ducks were caught, they discovered one had escaped them. George — he had worked at the hotel for many years — came to Bob, who was on the premises then, saying that he had found the duck. This all happened late in the evening, the same day as the great duck hunt.

Bob said, "Let's make a joke out of this and spook some of the people around here."

As Bob tells the story, he had it all worked out with George. George had the duck up on the third floor, and Bob would be at the front desk about ten minutes before mid-

Bob Ratcliffe, Sr., Palm Beach Shores police officer, with Mr. MacArthur shortly before Mr. Mac's death.

Permission: Bob Ratcliffe, Sr. (1977).

night. A girl named Elvira was working at the hotel front desk at that time.

Well, Bob was standing by, as promised, chatting with Elvira at the front desk. Their conversation concerned the duck hunt.

Elvira said, "I got kinda used to those ducks being around here. I don't know why they had to go."

Bob said, "You know, as mysterious as this hotel is and the crazy things that happen around here, you never know. That elevator could come down — and there could be a duck on it!"

"Yeah, sure," Elvira scoffed.

The clock struck midnight, and George put the duck on the elevator and pressed the button to the lobby.

When the elevator doors opened, there was the duck — quack, quack, quacking away.

Elvira's eyes widened to the size of silver dollars. She ran from behind the desk and out the front door. Meanwhile, Bob claims nobody has seen hide nor hair of Elvira since.

While the duck hunt took our minds off the passing of The Skipper briefly, we learned that there was to be no funeral in the accepted sense of the word; Mr. Mac wanted to spare his friends and relatives the inconvenience of attending a funeral, since it might mean appointments cancelled and flying overnight to arrive. Then, he willed his body to medical research, all very neat and tidy.

At the time of his death, he owned 45 companies and employed about 15,000 people. His Bankers Life and Casualty Company was the second largest in the world, and he was the sole stockholder in the Citizens Bank and Trust Company, the second largest bank in Illinois. Add to that 61 buildings in New York City, 100,000 acres of Florida land, hotels, golf courses, paper mills, farms, utility firms, oil wells, real estate firms, restaurants, a car rental firm, advertising agency — and the liquor company, from whence came the famous MacArthur Scotch; truly it was a mighty empire to contemplate.

Nevertheless, despite all of this wealth, I sensed dramatic changes would take place at the Colonnades — Mr. Mac's own personal playground; and I was right. Nothing was the same.

A few weeks went by. Rumors were flying around the hotel that said the hotel was going to be closed for the summer — probably sometime around May or June — to refurbish the place. Well, heaven knows, it needed it. Then, Mr. K came to see me, saying, "Bob, would you like to stay around for the summer and help us out? We'll keep you on the payroll."

It was nice of him to ask, but I said, "I'm a bartender — not a handyman." I thanked him, though, for the offer and told him I'd most likely be leaving the hotel. About a week later, I turned in my resignation. I had decided to go back to Cape Cod and spend the summer.

Upon my return to Florida in the fall, I went to the hotel and spoke to Mr. K about working there. He offered me a job at the tiki bar on the ocean. So far as the hotel went, they really hadn't done much. Oh, there was fresh paint, some new carpet, some badly needed work in the kitchen. Structurally, though, it was the same old place — about to fall down. But I'd always liked the tiki bar; it had a sense of fun and freedom about it. I took the job.

I did enjoy working out there again. It felt good to be back on the property again, almost like coming home, except it just wasn't the same without Mr. Mac. The hotel had lost its character. Mr. Mac *was* the hotel's character.

Sometimes, as I spent that last season at the hotel, I remembered things he had said to me, and I'd smile.

Once he had told me, "Any man who knows how much

Tiki bar, located on the ocean behind the Colonnades Beach Hotel.

Property of Bob Sanford (1978).

money he's worth isn't worth anything."

Another time: "If I wanted people to know how much money I have, I would paste my financial statement up on the wall."

He was there in that respect still. But the Colonnades Beach Hotel would never be the same again — without him.

Chapter 11

Where Have All the Players Gone?

Twenty-one years have come and gone since I first walked through those big glass doors at the Colonnades Beach Hotel. But I remember it all — as if it might have been yesterday.

I'm still a bartender, constantly reminding people about who John D. MacArthur was. I'm always telling the funny stories associated with Mr. Mac and the hotel. People love to hear these stories over and over. It's almost as if they wish they could bring him back and do it all over again.

Every once in awhile I get in my car and drive over to Palm Beach Shores just to see what's changed and what hasn't. Inevitably, I wind up parked in front of what is now just an empty parcel of land with a fence all around it. In 1989, after one of the floors on the second story of the main building collapsed, the town ordered the MacArthur Foundation to either renovate the building or knock it down. And so, in February 1990, demolition began and was quickly completed. Still the property itself is enormously valuable. In 1988 its value was figured at $25 million, for which Mr. Mac originally paid only $750,000.

It's an eerie feeling, seeing that property completely

empty. As a rule, I get out of my car and look at the ocean behind it, reflecting on all the great times I had working here, all the interesting people I met, and all the people with whom I worked. I remember too the big conventions and parties. But most of all, I remember The Skipper and how he reminded us all of who we were. Though he ran the ship, we had to be the best crew possible on a dime and a dance, as the saying goes.

Recently I learned that a deal has been finalized with the Marriott Ownership Resorts to develop a five-building oceanfront resort on 20 acres that once housed the world-renowned Colonnades Beach Hotel. The project is valued at $100 million, almost as much as the $147.4 million total assessed value of all existing property in Palm Beach Shores. Sometime in early 1996, Marriott will break ground for the resort complex which will encompass 313 condominiums, tennis courts, swimming pools and a croquet lawn. At long last, the Colonnades property will come alive again.

All of which made me think of the people with whom I once worked and what had happened to them. The list proved to be short; many of them had passed on. But I did manage to contact some of them.

I spoke with Molly Campany at her condo in Palm Beach Shores. We reminisced together for about three hours. It was good to see her again and talk with her after all these year.

I ran into Mary, my cocktail waitress, and she assured me that she was doing well. I was pleased about that.

I found out that Jack Penrose, who bartended for me, was working somewhere on Florida's west coast.

One who I see quite often is Cooper. Coop worked for Mr. Mac at the hotel for many years; he was involved mainly with the on-going construction projects outside the hotel. In the old days, I'd see him early in the morning when I came to

The vacant property where the Colonnades Beach Hotel was located, as it is today.

Property of Bob Sanford (February 1995).

work. Coop would be busy on a ladder or up on one of the roofs. He'd always give me a big wave and yell, "Hey, Bob, another great day!"

"Sure is, Coop" would be my response. Then, I'd add, "Keep up the good work!"

Nowadays I see Coop at my supermarket in Palm Beach Gardens. We always talk for a few minutes — always about Mr. Mac and the hotel.

Phil, Mr. Mac's private pilot, is still around. I caught up with him recently, and what a pleasure it was to see him again.

As for Mr. K, well, he met a tragic and untimely death — in the hotel he had done so much for. We'd had a black out at the hotel. Mr. K was trying to locate the elevator to figure out its position when he fell down the elevator shaft and died instantly He was 38-years-old.

I'll never forget that date — July 3, 1985. To this day, I have trouble believing that such a terrible thing could happen to anyone.

I have tried, over the years, to put my days, and the others who worked at the Colonnades Beach Hotel in perspective.

Mr. Mac once said, "When I'm gone I hope people will forget about me."

Without disturbing Mr. Mac's wishes, as far as I'm concerned: He lost . . . Those of us who knew him, those people who have been blessed by the John D. and Catherine T. MacArthur Foundation will never forget him.

Chapter 12

A Giant Shadow

It has been said that there are no great men — just ordinary men doing great things. If this is true, then John D. MacArthur was one of those men. He cast a giant shadow. Though it has been 18 years since his passing, his shadow hovers over Florida, in this case, reminding us always of the wonderful things he made possible while he lived.

This is especially true of Florida's northern Palm Beach County. One of MacArthur's most successful enterprises was the founding and building of Palm Beach Gardens on his vast real estate holdings there. Working as a team, Mr. Mac's wife Catherine chose the names of the streets which, I think, is a rather nice touch. Palm Beach Gardens is a thriving, attractive and prosperous community, a fitting tribute to the man who made it all possible. Currently Palm Beach Gardens occupies 54-square miles of land and has a population of 30,046. According to the University of Florida's Bureau of Economics and Business Research, by 2010, the population should escalate to 82,000.

MacArthur's own Holiday Inn and the three-championship-course J.D.M. Country Club (now Ballen Isles) was the home of PGA Headquarters, until it moved to the adjacent

This portion of MacArthur Boulevard is now a thriving housing development named after Mrs. MacArthur.

Property of Bob Sanford (1995).

PGA National Golf & Country Club.

Meanwhile and of most importance, is the John D. and Catherine T. MacArthur Foundation. The original papers were typed at the MacArthur apartment in the Colonnades Beach Hotel, Singer Island, Florida. While he was at it, Mr. Mac also created another foundation — Retirement Research Foundation which is quite small when compared to the John D. and Catherine T. MacArthur Foundation. But the Retirement Research Foundation is still to this day the largest foundation in the United States devoted exclusively to the problems of Senior Citizens.

Then, there's the John D. MacArthur Beach State Park. Mr. Mac went skinny dipping there, and he considered it the "best damn beach" anywhere. He always thought that this would be a great place for preserving nature — indigenous plants, trees, animals, flowers and, of course, the land. In 1980, the John D. and Catherine T. MacArthur Foundation donated this 82 acres of prime undeveloped oceanfront property in Palm Beach County for this purpose. The land appraised at more than $22 million .At the same time, the State of Florida, County of Palm Beach, purchased 273 adjoining acres from the foundation.

The two parcels formed the John D. MacArthur Beach State Park. The gift and sale were made with only conservation in mind, nothing more. In 1983, after several development options were studied and presented to the public for scrutiny and comment, the key principals decided on parking, visitor capacity and construction activities. In August of that same year, Governor Bob Graham and the Florida Cabinet approved the master plan; and what Mr. Mac had envisioned was about to become a reality.

In 1988, construction began on the John D. MacArthur State Park; it opened officially on Saturday, November 28, 1989.

Upon entering the park, two very distinct things are to be seen: one is a sculpture of John D. MacArthur, done by Margo McMahon from Chicago. Since Ms. McMahon had never met Mr. Mac and was unfamiliar with the area, Molly Campany, who was Mr. Mac's faithful helper for so many years, was asked to assist Ms. McMahon in capturing the essence of MacArthur. The bust of Mr. Mac was done from photographs Molly had in her possession.

Another aspect of interest as you approach the 4,000-square-foot building, where seashells, fish, plants, etc., indigenous to that area of Florida are displayed, is a sign in big letters, reading: WILLIAM T. KIRBY. And, indeed, Kirby was of importance in John D. and Catherine MacArthur's lives.

Kirby was a longtime associate of Mr. MacArthur. Kirby's shining hour came when he asked Mr. Mac, "Would you want the bulk of your fortune thrown into the hands of bureaucrats or people you know and trust?"

"I'll do what I do best. I'll make it, and after I'm dead, you guys will have to learn how to spend it." The Skipper had no intention of trying to manage his estate from the grave.

On several occasions, I have visited the park, a beautiful place with nature trails, undisturbed beaches for swimming, a quiet place to relax and feel at ease with oneself. And I never have failed to think of Mr. Mac and his friend talking about the future. What a glorious future it has been and will continue to be for years to come!

**Sculpture of John D. MacArthur at the MacArthur
State Beach Park, Singer Island, Florida.**

Photo property of Bob Sanford (1995).

Chapter 13

Questions Most Often Asked of Me

When folks find out that I once worked for John D. MacArthur questions abound. Here are the questions I'm most often asked.

"Was he a friendly man?"

Yes. He loved people, no question about it. He was a great communicator and a good storyteller. On many occasions, I saw him greeting hotel guests in the coffee shop as they came in for breakfast. Often times, he'd hold long conversations with total strangers.

"Did he own the McArthur Dairy?"

No. But it was easy to see why people might think he did, since Mr. Mac owned so much property in the area, bordering on Lake Okeechobee. However, this is an easy one, since the McArthur of the dairy people is spelled differently than Mr. Mac's last name.

"Did he really try to bring Disneyland to Palm Beach County?

Yes, he did, in the early 1960s. Mr. Mac entered into a business venture with the National Broadcasting Company and Radio Corporation of America. The group contacted Walt Disney about a joint business venture to bring Disneyland to Palm Beach County. Feasibility studies were done and proved favorable. However, as time wore on Walt Disney's brother, Roy, entered the picture, and from that point on the venture went down hill, for what reason it's not known. It's hard to imagine what obstacles kept Mr. Mac from succeeding. However, as one and all know, Disney doesn't like to share ownership of much of anything. Perhaps that had something to do with it. Nonetheless, this is just my guess. Regardless, Mr. Mac did have the vision to try.

"I've heard he was a dirty old man; was he?"

The way he carried on with women, one would have to say, "Yes." But it always seemed to be done in fun. Still and all, it was unacceptable conduct by modest standards.

"Did he live like a rich man?"

As the story goes, he tried to live high and mighty — just once. He had a big house outside of Chicago. He hired four servants and a man to manicure the lawn. However, it wasn't long before Mr. Mac figured out that this was all wrong for him. He'd go out of town on business, and upon his return, he'd discover that the servants didn't show up, or they'd polished off all of his whiskey. He decided the house was more trouble than it was worth.

"What do you know about the banyan trees located off Northlake Boulevard at the entrance to MacArthur Boulevard?"

Back in the early 1960s, these trees were uprooted from their original location to be planted at the entrance of Mr. Mac's new city, Palm Beach Gardens. The moving of the trees was a project riddled with problems too numerous to mention. However, Mr. Mac spent thousands of dollars trying to accomplish the feat. One of the trees was a male, and the other was a female. He had them planted side by side and actually had a ceremony with a local minister present.

When the minister asked Mr. Mac about the prayer he should say, Mr. Mac replied, "It wouldn't hurt to ask God for a little rain."

Some people questioned his sanity in spending so much money the moving of those trees. Mr. Mac's answer, "I can buy anything but age. These trees will be the centerpiece of our entrance, and while we could have planted smaller trees, I wouldn't be around 80 years from now to see it as it should be."

These trees are now over 100-years-old. They are a beautiful centerpiece for all of us to admire. These trees earned Mr. Mac the nickname, "Banyan Mac."

"Did Mr. MacArthur have a humorous side?"

Well, you've seen some of it in the pages of this story. As interesting and colorful as Mr. Mac was, it was his spontaneous humor that helped to make him bigger than life.

"Was he a happy man?"

This is the most asked question. And it is the hardest to

The two banyan trees that Mr. MacArthur had transplanted at the entrance to his dream city, Palm Beach Gardens, in the early 1960s. The trees are located on MacArthur Boulevard off Northlake Boulevard.

Property of Bob Sanford (1995).

answer. But I do believe he was a happy man. He had everything he wanted and more. Since he never cared for the material aspects of life, he was free, so to speak. And this makes for happiness. He could do what he wanted to do when he wanted to do it. He took pleasure in the long lines of people who came to see him every day. He loved the chance to shake a hand and share a joke. He also loved nature — birds, flowers, trees, animals of all kinds. Oh, and let's not forget those ducks and that daily feeding. How he did enjoy those ducks! So, yes, on the whole I think he was a happy man. Just playing the game made him happy — and, of course, winning — and no one can dispute that he didn't win at the game he loved best, making money.

"Is Jamie MacArthur, from the television series *Hawaii Five-0* — he played the role of Sgt. Dano — related to John D. MacArthur?

Yes. Jamie MacArthur is the adopted son of Charles MacArthur, John's brother, and Helen Hayes.

Chapter 14

Upfront & Personal with Mr. Mac

O ver the years I've saved and collected a few items that reflect the John D. MacArthur I knew. One of them is the INTER-OFFICE CORRESPONDENCE printed below, which he wrote to me during the time I worked for him.

INTER-OFFICE CORRESPONDENCE

Send to: Mr. Bob Sanford - Bar Manager   From: John MacArthur   Date: Sept. 15, 1975

Subject:

I discussed the advisability of the staff drinking in the hotel.

All hotels ask their employees to do their drinking at other places. However, there is no rule that cannot be broken. If someone is soliciting business they should be able to buy the prospect a drink or two at our hotel.

As owner of the hotel I will occasionally buy a few drinks for friends and staff members.   I will expect the same treatment as any customer and will sign a check.   I would expect any employee who entertains to put the name of the prospect on the check and sign it.   This will enable you to keep track of your inventory.

JDM:gew

152A

Another item that I believe reflects the man is a prayer Mr. Mac carried with him everywhere. Molly Campany told me that when Mr. Mac showed it to her, he said, "This might well be my epitaph — but I'd have to change some of the words around." Still, it is a glimpse of the inner man and his upbringing:

A MAN'S PRAYER

Teach men that sixty minutes make an hour, sixteen ounces a pound, a hundred cents a dollar. Help me to live so that I can lie down at night with a clear conscience and unhaunted by the faces of those to whom I may have brought pain. Grant that I may earn my meal ticket on the square, and in earning it I may do unto others as I would have them do unto me. Deafen me to the jingle of tainted money. Blind me to the faults of other fellows and reveal to me my own. Guide me so that each night when I look across the table at my wife, who has been a blessing to me, I will have nothing to conceal. Keep me young enough to laugh with little children and sympathetic so as to be considerate of old age. And comes the day of darkening shades make the ceremony short and the epitaph simple: "Here lies a man."

To me, this epitomizes Mr. Mac perfectly. I do believe he tried to live his life along these lines, and I wouldn't be a bit surprised, if the prayer wasn't handed down to him from his father.

After Mr. Mac died, personal friends took to gathering on his birthday. At the fourth annual gathering on March 6, 1981, here's a toast, written by Lonnie Cargill

A TOAST TO "MR. MAC"

Now here's to one big winner
Who knew how to play the game
For he played with skill and wisdom
John MacArthur was his name.

He also played with kindness
And with charm in each command
And he made you proud and happy
When he reached to shake your hand.

Now other poker players
Sit around the same big table.
They're more sophisticated,
And they think they're much more able.

But won't you please remind them
Just in case their memory slips
It was our friend John MacArthur
Who provided all their chips.

Mr. Mac's favorite music was *September Song*. When I hear the song I always remember one line from the song — in particular, "One hasn't got time for the waiting game."

He was driven by a need to excel, and, yes, he didn't have time for the "waiting game".

But I also never forget the words that precede this line. They are "But the days grow short when you reach September". I do believe that's what kept him going in his last years when bad health was catching up with him. Time was growing short, and he loved life so much, he crammed into each and every day far more than his strength allowed.

I am so pleased I was able to be a part of those days. It was an unforgettable experience.

Mr. Mac, I miss you . . .

Sources

The MacArthur Heritage, A Story of an American Family, Barbara Graymont and John F. Taylor, John D. and Catherine T. MacArthur Foundation

The Palm Beach Post, West Palm Beach, Florida

The MacArthur Legacy, The First Ten Years, The MacArthur Foundation

Palm Beach Gardens History Highlights, Patricia Smith

City of Palm Beach Gardens and Patricia Smith

The Penalty of Leadership

John D. says a friend once passed along these words to him, and he's kept them handy ever since:

In every field of human endeavor, he that is first must perpetually live in the white light of publicity.

Whether the leadership be vested in man or in a manufactured product, emulation and envy are ever at work. In art, in literature, in music, in industry, the reward and the punishment are always the same. The reward is widespread recognition; the punishment, fierce denial and detraction.

Jealousy does not protrude its forked tongue at the artist who produces a commonplace painting. Whatsoever you write, or paint, or play, or sing, or build, no one will strive to surpass or slander you unless your work be stamped with the seal of genius.

The leader is assailed because he is a leader, and the effort to equal him is merely added proof of that leadership. Failing to equal or excel, the follower seeks to depreciate and to destroy — but only confirms once more the superiority of that which he strives to supplant. There is nothing new in this. It is as old as the world and as old as the human passions.

If the leader truly leads, he remains the leader. That which is good or great makes itself known, no matter how loud the clamour of denial. That which deserves to live lives.

— Author unknown

About the Author

Bob Sanford is a native of Massachusetts. He began working as a bartender on Cape Cod in 1966. He moved to Tampa, Florida, in 1971, where he was employed as beverage manager at the Red Carpet Inn. In 1975, a telephone call from the Colonnades Beach Hotel brought him to the Palm Beach area, where he worked for fifteen years on Singer Island. Currently he works as a bartender in Palm Beach Gardens, Florida. Now, 21 years after his first meeting with John D. MacArthur, he is determined to keep his memory of Mr. Mac alive.

John D. MacArthur:
A View From the Bar
(A Memoir)

by Bob Sanford

Additional copies of *John D. MacArthur: A View From the Bar* can be had by doing any one of the following:

— calling, toll free, 1-800-356-9315, Visa/MC/Amex accepted

— faxing, toll free, 1-800-242-0036, Visa/MC/Amex accepted

— sending $15.00, plus $3.00 shipping and handling, plus applicable sales tax to Rainbow Books, Inc., P. O. Box 430, Highland City, FL 33846-0430.

— asking your local bookseller to order ISBNumber 1-56825-036-3

This entire page, as well as the cover of *John D. MacArthur: A View From the Bar*, can be modified to reflect your large-quantity, special purchase. Contact the Publisher, Betty Wright, at the above address for more information.